'Consciousness' has always been an important concept in the science of behavior, even during the years when it was avowedly banned by Behaviorism. It is in terms of 'consciousness' that the biological and psychological notions of 'stimulus' and 'response' are differentiated, and that 'learning' has been and continues to be defined. What is thus required is an explicit, independent, physicalistic definition of 'conscious experience,' abstracted from common scientific usage. Dr. Kendon Smith builds up such an abstraction and offers a much needed definition to accord with it.

Consciousness is implicitly central to psychology in particular. The evidence is that consciousness is a physical and essentially "public" event. It records internal behavior as it does external. This book therefore concludes by recommending something of a methodological reorientation in psychology. Its suggestion is for a rigorous "introspectional behaviorism," in which careful introspectional report supplements external observation. By the provision of an account of internal as well as of external behavior, the entire flux of stimulus and response would be made available for scientific scrutiny.

Kendon R. Smith was educated at the University of Minnesota and Princeton University. He has published numerous and influential articles in scientific journals such as the Journal of Experimental Psychology, the Psychological Review and Science. He is Professor of Psychology at the University of North Carolina at Greensboro and spent last year at the University of Turku in Finland.

Behavior and Conscious Experience
A Conceptual Analysis

For Helen

Behavior and Conscious Experience
A Conceptual Analysis

KENDON SMITH

Ohio University Press   Athens, Ohio

CONTENTS

Behavior and Conscious Experience
A Conceptual Analysis

I

INTRODUCTION

WE SHOULD BE concerned, I think, by the vagueness of the concepts used in the study of behavior. The ideas employed by the more derivative of the "behavioral sciences" are especially hazy; but even those relatively fundamental concepts which are used in the branches of biology and psychology addressing themselves to the basic problems of behavior are far from clear. This lack of precision is not necessarily fatal; scientific progress can still be made. All the same, the history of science attests plainly to the fact that any investigative effort gets along better if it knows exactly what it is talking about.

The present monograph grew out of the feeling so expressed. It inquires into what we mean by the terms 'stimulus,' 'response,' 'learning,' and 'conscious experience.' When I say "we," I refer to biologists, psychologists, and other scientists who deal with behavior. When I ask what we mean, I am not asking merely what we *think of* whenever we use a given term (although it is, of course, necessary to start out with that question in mind). I am asking what we *really* mean when we use the term: What is the fundamental nature of the object or phenomenon to which that term is customarily applied?

With such an objective in view, it plainly behooves me

to say something at once about what might be called the "metaphysical assumptions" of the present volume, for they will certainly be implicit in much that remains to be said. These assumptions have in fact already been set forth and defended (Smith 1958, 1959) *; but they will be restated briefly in the two sections just below: "Basic Premises: Naturalism, Reductionism, and Determinism," and "Basic Premises: Conscious Experience." With those two sections, the present, introductory chapter will come to a close.

The four chapters which follow the present one will be devoted directly to the analyses of the concepts at issue. The first two of those chapters will be concerned with 'stimulus' and 'response'; and, as will be seen, it has proved advantageous to consider the two terms as a pair, but as a pair differing in significance as between biologists and psychologists. The third of the four chapters will deal with 'learning,' and the fourth will attempt a definition of 'conscious experience.'

Emerging from the analyses provided by these four chapters are, I believe, some fairly important implications. They have to do with the relationship of biology to psychology, with the essential nature of the psychologist's task, and with certain ways in which the psychologist's task might be approached more profitably. The closing chapter of the volume will attempt to set down those implications.

Basic Premises: Naturalism, Reductionism, and Determinism

The fundamental assumption upon which the present essays rest is that of naturalism (or "physical realism," or "materialism"). Naturalism is the view, widely held

* Full details of sources referred to in the text will be found at the end of each chapter.

among the sciences, that not only the inanimate world
but the animate world as well is a purely natural phenomenon; nowhere in the universe is the preternatural to
be found. Put another way, naturalism is "the doctrine
that the whole of what exists is constituted of matter and
its local motions, . . . 'physical' in the literal sense that
all its constituents are among the subject matter of physics" (Williams 1944: 418).

That which is alive is, in this view, readily distinguish-
able by purely naturalistic criteria from that which is
not: "a 'living object' is an object which will absorb
substances from some environment and synthesize from
them a replication of each of the substances which comprise that object" (Smith 1958: 415). Being a part of the
physical world, "a living object is . . . exactly what De-
mocritus said it was: a swarm of particles in space"
(Smith 1958: 415). The fact that the particles may be
packets of energy, rather than the hard billiard balls of
classical mechanics, does not at all change the principle
involved (cf. Williams 1944: 425–426).

It is further assumed that there are, in this naturalistic world, no true "emergents."

> Patently, a "whole" consists of parts in a configuration,
> and such a configuration will have properties not pos-
> sessed by the individual parts. This is not to say, how-
> ever, that the characteristics of the whole could not be
> deduced from a knowledge of the characteristics of the
> individual parts *and of their relationships to one an-
> other.* A thorough understanding of hydrogen atoms
> and oxygen atoms, plus an awareness of how such
> atoms are disposed in a molecule of water, should cer-
> tainly lead to the inference that molecules of water
> would have just a middling attraction for one another
> and would therefore constitute, in quantity, a liquid.
> Under such circumstances, it seems pointless to talk
> about "emergent wetness.". . . [A] defensible reduc-

tionism would point out that the living object, specifically, is a collection of basic particles; that these particles behave in a lawful fashion; that, being in a certain
momentary configuration, they can behave in only one
way, and the next configuration follows inevitably (and
from this still another, and so on). The behavior of the
component particles is completely predictable from a
knowledge of their properties and of their interrelationships; but the behavior of the whole configuration
is exactly identical with the behavior of these particles.
Thus, the properties of the living object may be de-
duced from a knowledge of the properties of the particles which compose it and of their interrelationships.
In this context, there is no escaping the truth of Bergmann's trenchant dictum: "Logically and in principle
. . . reduction is a certainty. . . . Philosophies which
deny or even doubt that are simply silly (1953: 442)."
[Smith 1958: 417]

A naturalistic world is, in consonance with what has
just been said, a deterministic world. 'Determinism' is a
misleading word; to many, it implies something like fa-
talism. In actual fact, the meaning of the word is simple
and not very threatening. Determinism is merely the
doctrine of strict cause and effect. It argues that the
cosmos, in all of its ramifications, has flowed inevitably
from one instantaneous state to the next, since the beginning of time; and that it will continue to do so into the
indefinite future. It is, of course, a corollary of this view
that human behavior is a cause-and-effect phenomenon,
and thus that every human choice is inevitable. The validity of this corollary is, however, a matter of everyday
experience. If one imagines himself as exactly the same
individual in exactly same situation in which he once
made a choice, he will find it impossible to imagine himself as now making a choice different from the one he
made upon that occasion. The original choice flowed from
its circumstances, and precisely the same circumstances

would produce precisely the same choice again. One is always free, of course, to do as he chooses; but the choice itself is clearly inevitable.

The doctrine of strict determinism has been questioned repeatedly, during the twentieth century, in terms of an unwarranted extension of Heisenberg's principle of indeterminacy. Even in the unlikely event that that extension should happen to be veridical after all, however, the essence of the matter would remain unchanged. Determinism would merely become probablistic. Living objects, furthermore, would remain so gross as to be still virtually completely predictable, in any case (Smith 1958: 418–419).

It is, of course, imperative that the naturalistic conception of life account for the phenomenon of conscious experience. Although it has often done so by postulating some form of psychophysical parallelism, there seem to be well-nigh conclusive arguments against parallelism and in favor of physical monism. The question of the nature of conscious experience is, in fact, one which needs a more extended treatment than have the issues considered in the present section. Accordingly, the entire following section is devoted to its discussion.

Basic Premises: Conscious Experience

'Conscious experience,' 'consciousness,' and 'awareness' are all taken here as essentially synonymous. For the time being, furthermore, their common meaning is specified merely ostensively. They refer, then, to such phenomena as "sensations," "perceptions," "thoughts," "images," "dreams," "wishes," and "emotions." This usage is meant to be entirely commonplace.

In dealing with the naturalistic conception of consciousness, it is convenient to divide the present section into two subsections. The first of these will attempt to describe somewhat more carefully than is usual the nature of the phenomenon to be explained. The second will combine the picture derived from the first with the basic naturalistic postulate, and reach a conclusion as to the place of awareness in a purely physical world.

The Phenomenon To Be Explained. It is very difficult not to think of consciousness as an entity of some sort. Unless we are careful, we presume that there is within each of us still another sentient creature. That creature seems to know itself directly, and to be aware of the outside world through "messages" that come to it as sensations. So strong is this impression that many have accepted the presumed creature as real, and called it by such names as "the conscious mind," "the ego," or "the self."

All of this is, as K. S. Lashley remarked shortly before the end of his life, simply a tribute to poor introspection (Lashley 1958: 3). As has been insisted repeatedly by the most eminent of authorities (James 1896: 224ff., and 1904; Titchener 1929: 265–266; Lashley 1923, 1958; Boring 1933: 18–22), what we call 'consciousness' is absolutely nothing other than a flow of events: of sensation, of perception, of images, of thought, of impulse, of emotion. The title of James's paper of 1904 asked, for example, "Does 'Consciousness' Exist?"; and James concluded that—as an entity—consciousness did not; the core of "the self," James suggested, was the sensation of regular respiration. A half-century later, Lashley was equally emphatic:

> The only conclusion that can be derived from experience is that thought exists. No psychologist has ever discovered the thinker. . . . There are neither empirical nor logical grounds for assuming that the existence of consciousness implies a distinct entity which is in the relation to it of a knower or doer. . . . *No activity of mind is ever conscious.* . . . There are order and

arrangement, but there is no experience of the creation of that order. . . . If the organization were provided by a slide rule or by a digital computer, consciousness would give no indication of the fact nor any basis for denying it. [Lashley 1958: 3–4] . . . [Thus,] the problem of the content of experience boils down to accounting for the character of sensations. [Lashley 1958: 12]

The totality of what is being said in such passages is not easy to convey. At the same time, it is most important actually to convey it. The following conceptualization is accordingly offered in an attempt to do so.

There have long been "motor theories of consciousness," and they have assumed various forms. In one form, "sensation" is regarded, in the orthodox manner, as the direct consequence of afferent impulses' having reached the brain from a sense organ. "Perceiving," however, is viewed as fine muscular activity, as minute changes in tension, posture, or bodily orientation; such muscular activity is supposed to stimulate receptors in the muscles, tendons, and joints, and thus to arouse its own pattern of sensation—which is reported as "perception." "Thinking" or "imaging" follows much the same paradigm: muscular behavior of small amplitude but significant topography arouses a sequence of sensory events, and the individual experiences "thoughts" or "images." "Wanting," similarly, is the implicit beginning of explicit behavior; the individual experiences the corresponding muscular sensations, and speaks of a "wish." Much or all of this inner behavior is learned, and is thus mediated by the associational pathways of the brain. It is crucial to note, however, that no conscious experience is supposed to accompany the function of any associative pathway. The entire awareness of the individual is composed, in fact, of sensations. Some of these sensations are exteroceptive, some are interoceptive, and many are proprioceptive; but all are merely sensations.

The only true "self" is the literal, physical self constituted by the individual's body; and the individual knows
about that self on exactly the same basis as he knows
about the "external world."

Now, it is not argued just here that this view of consciousness is necessarily correct. It is, however, pointed
out that the view cannot be refuted introspectively. No
one has even thought of attempting such refutation; the
kind of evidence brought to bear has had to do with
curarization, muscle potentials, and the like. Such irref-
utability testifies plainly to the nature of the phenomenon that needs to be explained. It indicates quite clearly
that conscious experience is indeed not an entity, but
simply a process—a flow of events. From that flow of
events, the individual deduces his own existence, just as
surely as he does that of the rest of reality. "If all of
conscious experience is not sensation, it might just as
well be: consciousness simply happens" (Smith 1958:
420).

A Naturalistic Explanation of Consciousness.
Actually, the facts pointed out above were once, a century or so ago, fairly commonly recognized. At that same
point in time, there was an almost militant loyalty,
among scientists, to a strictly naturalistic *Weltan-
schauung.* And, finally, there existed a universal and un-
questioned assumption that material processes were one
thing and conscious experience quite another, that the
two were qualitatively entirely different.

It seemed to many at the time, and it has seemed to
many since, that the only resolution to this trio of premises was some sort of psychophysical parallelism. The
preferred variety has been that of epiphenomenalism. In
such a view, the organism remains a completely natural
object, a complex physicochemical system totally responsive to natural law. As it functions, nevertheless, it
generates consciousness as a by-product, as an "epiphe-

nomenon." That conscious experience has no function whatsoever; it is not "efficacious" in governing behavior. All of life would go on completely unchanged if awareness could be obliterated without infringing on organic integrity.

The principal objection to epiphenomenalism has always been that it is incredible. There has been some difficulty, over the years, in rationalizing that intuitive conviction; but rationalization has recently been attempted with some force. Thus,

> The question now arises [in connection with epiphenomenalism], however: who or what is *having* this experience? Certainly not the living object. . . . Its constituent particles remain untouched; it cannot be undergoing an experience of any kind. [Smith 1958: 420]

Experience is not experience unless it is happening to someone; and, if it *is* happening to someone, it is clearly not an epiphenomenon.

The same argument can be put more concretely; and Muller has so put it, with great cogency: "If this view [i.e., parallelism in general] were correct, the existence of consciousness, being only 'parallel,' could in no way affect our behavior. Hence we could not speak of it. Nor could we, for that matter, even think of it (for the conscious could no more than parallel the material side, and the latter could not be affected by the former)" (Muller 1955: 7). To the sophistry that we only *believe* we are responding to consciousness itself, when in reality we are responding to the physical event that generates consciousness, there is a simple reply: We are quite able to speak and think, not only about the stimuli and objects that arouse awareness, but about awareness *qua* awareness; we plainly do so when, for example, we describe the quality or the intensity of a conscious experience.

In his own discussion, Muller goes on directly, to state the obvious corollary: "It follows that the conscious phenomena *are* the physicochemical phenomena or, at least, some integrated portion of them" (Muller 1955: 7). If awareness is produced by natural events, as we know it to be; and if awareness produces in turn still other natural events, as we now see that it does; then there would appear to be no alternative to the view that awareness itself is a proper part of nature. This view is the doctrine of physical monism. It has been urged in recent years, not only by Muller, but by Feigl (1958, 1959, 1960), Lashley (1958), Pepper (1960), Langer (1962: 1–25), and Smart (1963: 92–105). It was espoused in the earlier paper (Smith 1958), and it is espoused here.

The full significance of physical monism is rather difficult to communicate. The difficulty arises out of the radical discrepancy between the true meaning of physical monism, on the one hand, and the traditional assumptions of both philosophy and common sense, on the other. In an effort to solve this communicational problem by main force, I wish now to emphasize as strongly as I can just what is being said here.

To say that consciousness is physical, then, is to say, flatly and unequivocally, that sensations, perceptions, and ideas are absolutely nothing more than, nor less than, nor different from, changes in the very substance of the brain. Thus, as I listen to a tone whose frequency is 500 cycles per second, I have a conscious experience; and this experience consists of, and is in every way identical with, a physical activity in the temporal lobe of my brain. Were you carefully to expose this area of my brain, and to inspect it with a still-to-be invented supermicroscope, you would see my experience of auditory sensation. It would not, of course, produce an auditory sensation in you: I am having the experience; you are merely watching it. Again, the same notion can be pushed one step further by now imagining that I am looking at a sunset and experiencing redness, and that you are scrutinizing my occipital lobe. There, you see my experience of redness. It does not, however, produce the experience of redness in you. Why should it? Electromagnetic waves of the spacing necessary to generate a reddish sensation are being radiated by the sunset—not by my experience of redness (cf. Pepper 1960).

Upon such a note, it is perhaps appropriate to close the present section. The section could be epitomized by saying that what we ordinarily refer to as 'consciousness' is simply a sequence of events to which we give such names as 'sensation,' 'perception,' and 'thought'; and by repeating that there is every reason to believe that those events are completely physical in nature. Within this framework of physical monism, all that remains to be said in the present volume will be lodged. Awareness—consciousness, conscious experience—will thus be treated throughout as a natural event, caused by antecedent natural events, and capable of giving rise in turn to other, consequent natural events.

To say that conscious experience is a physical event is, of course, merely to place it in a very broad category. Although it has perhaps been of some help in delimiting the concept to appeal to the usual ostensive definition, it should be noted that we still require a truly rigorous characterization of the notion of 'consciousness.' Chapter V of the present volume will attempt to provide such a characterization, as has already been indicated; but there is a certain reasonableness to dealing first with the concepts of 'stimulus' and 'response' and 'learning.' We shall accordingly go ahead now to scrutinize the latter concepts, continuing as we do so to regard 'consciousness' as a logically primitive term having simply a "pointing" definition.

REFERENCES

Bergmann, G. 1953. "Theoretical Psychology." In: Stone,
    C. P. (ed.) ; 1953; *Annual Review of Psychology*, Vol-
    ume 4; Annual Reviews, Stanford, California.
Boring, E. G. 1933. *The Physical Dimensions of Conscious-
    ness*. Century, New York and London.
Feigl, H. 1958. "The 'Mental' and the 'Physical.' " In:
    Feigl, H., M. Scriven, and G. Maxwell (eds.) ; *Minne-
    sota Studies in the Philosophy of Science*, Volume II:
    Concepts, Theories, and the Mind-Body Problem; Uni-
    versity of Minnesota Press, Minneapolis.
Feigl, H. 1959. "Philosophical Embarrassments of Psychol-
    ogy." *Amer. Psychologist, 14*, 115–128.
Feigl, H. 1960. "Mind-Body, *Not* a Pseudoproblem." In:
    Hook, S. (ed.) ; *Dimensions of Mind*; New York Uni-
    versity Press, New York.
James, W. 1896. *The Principles of Psychology*, Volume I.
    Holt, New York.
James, W. 1904. "Does 'Consciousness' Exist?" *J. Philos.
    Psychol. and Scientific Methods, 1*, 477–491.
Langer, S. K. 1962. *Philosophical Sketches*. Johns Hopkins
    Press, Baltimore.
Lashley, K. S. 1923. "The Behavioristic Interpretation of
    Consciousness: I and II." *Psychol. Rev., 30*, 237–272
    and 329–353.
Lashley, K. S. 1958. "Cerebral Organization and Behavior."
    In: Solomon, H. C., S. Cobb, and W. Penfield (eds.) ;
    The Brain and Human Behavior; Volume 36, *Research
    Publications of the Association for Research in Nerv-
    ous and Mental Disease*; William and Wilkins, Balti-
    more. Also, reprinted in: Beach, F. A., D. O. Hebb,
    C. T. Morgan, and H. W. Nissen (eds.) ; 1960; *The
    Neuropsychology of Lashley*; McGraw-Hill, New York.
Muller, H. J. 1955. "Life." *Science, 121*, 1–9.
Pepper, S. C. 1960. "A Neural-Identity Theory of Mind."
    In: Hook, S. (ed.) ; *Dimensions of Mind*; New York
    University Press, New York.

Smart, J. J. C. 1963. *Philosophy and Scientific Realism.* Humanities Press, New York.

Smith, K. 1958. "The Naturalistic Conception of Life." *Amer. Scientist, 46,* 413–423.

Smith, K. 1959. (Letter to the editor.) *Amer. Scientist, 47,* 139–140.

Titchener, E. B. 1929. *Systematic Psychology: Prolegomena.* Macmillan, New York.

Williams, D. 1944. "Naturalism and the Nature of Things." *Philos. Rev., 53,* 417–443.

II

THE CONCEPTS OF 'STIMULUS' AND 'RESPONSE' IN BIOLOGY

AS THE preceding chapter has already suggested, it is most convenient to regard the terms 'stimulus' and 'response' first from the viewpoint of the biologist and then from that of the psychologist. Accordingly, the present chapter will examine the concepts associated with those terms within biology; and the following chapter will scrutinize the analogous concepts within psychology.

The examination carried out by the present chapter may perhaps be of some direct value to biology itself; for, although 'stimulus' and 'response' are fundamental biological terms, there has been almost no analysis of the ideas for which they stand. In the present context, too, the examination should have a certain prefatory value. In gaining an understanding of the biological concepts of 'stimulus' and 'response,' we should go some way toward achieving insight into the corresponding psychological concepts—even though, as will become apparent, the latter notions represent major departures from the former.

Tacitly underlying this essay are the premises developed and defended in the last one. That is to say, we shall assume, throughout, a view of the living object which is naturalistic, reductionistic, and deterministic. The element of conscious experience will not figure explicitly in the present chapter; nevertheless, it is just as well to recall here that the position already adopted in this matter is that of physical monism—the view that the flow of conscious experience is completely identical with some inner physical process.

We might reasonably expect, in an examination of the concepts of 'stimulus' and 'response,' to deal first with the former notion and then with the latter. As one explores the literature, however, it soon becomes apparent that the procedure actually required is just the reverse. Almost invariably, biology defines 'stimulus' in terms of 'response.' The concept represented by the latter term is thus the more basic one, and the one with which analysis should in fact begin. In the discussion which follows, we shall accordingly consider first the biological idea of 'response' and then the biological idea of 'stimulus.'

'Response' in Biology

It will be helpful to begin our consideration with a brief discussion of 'response' as a generic term, and we shall do so. We shall thereafter go on to the biological conception itself, paying special attention to the idea of 'liberation of energy' and to the limitations which must be placed upon it if it is to be useful in our task of definition. Finally, we shall attempt, specifically in terms of the liberation of chemical energy by a living object, a rigorous characterization of the concept of 'response.'

'Response' as a Generic Term. The word 'response,' along with such essentially synonymous words as 'reaction' and 'behavior,' was undoubtedly acquired from the store of common speech; and it is worth noting at the outset that, in common speech itself, all of these words are used in an extremely broad and general fashion. Sometimes they convey a clear implication of consciousness and volition, as when we are said to respond to

a smile, react to a gesture, or behave well or badly. At
other times, when this implication of will and awareness
is lost, the words may still retain a distinct flavor of
spontaneity: thus, a seed "responds" to the sun, or an
explosive "reacts" to a mechanical disturbance, or an
engine "behaves" brilliantly. Finally, in perhaps more
cases than we realize, the words in question bear no sense
of spontaneity or conscious endeavor at all, but refer
instead to some essentially passive process. The leaves of
a tree, for example, "respond" to a passing breeze; or a
solution of silver chloride, exposed to the sun, "reacts" by
changing color; or the water in a channel "behaves" first
in one way and then in another, as the conformation of
the channel is altered.

The Biological Conception of 'Response.'   Considering the latitude with which these terms are employed in
common speech, we might expect them to be used rather
broadly in biology also. We might anticipate, for instance, that a report on the "behavior" of amoeba
would include, among other things, data on patterns of
distortion in the plasmagel, information concerning the
degree of viscosity of the plasmasol, and an account of
the staining properties of the nuclear inclusions. Such
expectations are, of course, not fulfilled; for 'response,'
'reaction,' and 'behavior' have a unique significance
for the biologist. When he uses these words, he means not
merely *anything* that happens in a living object; but,
rather, *something special* that happens in a living object.

Now, it is a striking fact that, in reading the biological
literature, we are virtually forced to infer for ourselves
what this something special might be. 'Behavior,' 'reaction,' and 'response' are almost always employed in a
logically primitive fashion, being used without definition
both in narration and in the stated meanings of such
terms as 'stimulus' and 'excitability' (e.g., Bard 1935:
874; Best and Taylor 1950: 903). It is true that we can

find occasional attempts at explicit definition (cf. Verworn 1916: 39; Halliburton and McDowall 1935: 10, 23; Scheer 1948: 39ff.; Heilbrunn 1952: 564–568) ; but it is also true that these efforts tend to be casual and their products overly simplified. Thus, we find 'response' equated unreservedly with such terms as 'liberation of energy,' 'transformation of energy,' 'spontaneous activity,' or 'changes of the vital processes.' As the next few paragraphs will attempt to show, these terms are much too broad and inclusive to furnish a valid definition.

Perhaps the prime example of excessive breadth is the phrase, 'changes of the vital processes.' The phrase is Max Verworn's (1916: 39), and Verworn made a real attempt to place certain limitations upon the concept of 'vital processes'; nevertheless, the expression remains patently overinclusive. Much the same sort of thing can be said about 'spontaneous activity.' What is meant by 'spontaneous'? At worst, the word refers to something mystical. At best, it refers merely to the liberation of internal energy, and it might better say so directly.

'Transformation of energy,' to consider another possibility, undoubtedly embraces every event to which a biologist would apply the label of 'response.' Unfortunately, however, it also embraces many others. An amoeba basking in the sun, for instance, becomes warmer as it transforms photic energy into thermal; but, clearly, this transformation does not constitute a biological response. Again, it is possible that some living cells have piezoelectrical properties, so that they are able to convert mechanical energy into electrical. To a physicist, such a conversion would indeed be a response. To a biologist, on the other hand, it would not be. The biologist excludes from *his* category of 'response' all instances of mere transduction and, therefore, a great many cases of transformation of energy.

The foregoing logic suggests that we discard from the class of events of 'transformation of energy' all those which represent only the *transduction* of energy. If we follow this suggestion, we shall have left as a residue the class of 'liberation of energy'; and, as we have already seen, it is often urged that 'response' be defined in precisely these terms. Such a formulation, in terms of the expenditure of energy from funds within the living object itself, has a strong intuitive appeal; and it undoubtedly constitutes a step in the right direction. All the same, it is still much too sweeping. It needs to be narrowed and qualified; and the limitations which must be placed upon it are really quite considerable. Accordingly, a new section will be devoted to a discussion of these limitations.

Limitations upon 'Liberation of Energy' as the Definition of 'Response.' As one explores the significance of the phrase, 'liberation of energy,' the first reservation to be placed upon it as a definition of 'response' becomes, perhaps, fairly obvious. We shall now consider that reservation.

We need to recall that all objects, including living objects, possess measurable stores of potential energy simply by virtue of their relationships with other objects. For example, a human being in upright posture upon the earth constitutes a fair repository of the potential energy of position; and the human skin, pressed upon and held under tension by an external instrument, becomes another, more modest, reservoir of energy. This energy is easily released. If the individual trips and falls to the ground, or if the instrument is removed and the skin rebounds, liberation has occurred. It is noteworthy, however, that we do not view such an expenditure of energy as a response. We are not responding when we fall involuntarily, or when we allow a bit of skin to restore itself to normal position. It appears, then, that the first limita-

tion upon 'liberation of energy' as the definition of 'response' is this: *The biological conception of 'response'
does not include the liberation of potential energy maintained in a living object by the presence of an external
agency.*

The second reservation is symmetrical with the first:
*The liberation of potential energy maintained in a living
object by the action of a purely internal agency is also
not a part of the biological concept of 'response.'* Less
self-evident than the first qualification, this one is nevertheless susceptible of ready confirmation. Two examples
may serve to make the point:

(1) The first concerns ingestion in amoeba. This is
an activity which is regarded as a response. It would
appear, however, that such a view depends entirely
upon the assumption that ingestion is more than the
mere liberation of potential energy maintained by an
internal agency. Thus, if it should be discovered to-
morrow that the elaborate routine of ingestion reflects
merely a preexisting tension in the protoplasmic membrane, a weakening of the membrane at the point of
contact with a particle of food, and a consequent mechanical squeezing and extrusion of the contents of the
cell—if it should be discovered, in a word, that this
activity represents simply the expenditure of potential
energy, internally maintained—then we should certainly dismiss ingestion summarily from the category
of 'response.'

(2) The second example has to do with neural conduction. As we all know, such conduction is still something
of a mystery; indeed, there is a real doubt as to
whether the transmission of a single impulse should
even be called a "response." If it should be established,
however, that neural conduction consists in fact of no
more than a passive breakdown of the neural mem-

brane, a breakdown which allows ions of opposing
charges to rush together in such a fashion that the
membrane is further eroded away, thus allowing more
ions to rush together, thus causing more erosion, and
so on—if it should be determined, that is to say, that a
single neural impulse represents merely the liberation
of internal potential energy—then the terminological
uncertainty would immediately be resolved: the conduction of a neural impulse would *not* be a response.
The restitution of the neural membrane, or the work
performed by the sodium pump, might well qualify;
but not the mere liberation of the potential energy
inherent in stored, opposing electrical charges.

Examples might be multiplied, but these would seem to
suffice in establishing the principle in question.

We have now cited two major reservations upon the
definition of 'response' as 'liberation of energy.' The
first says that the liberation of potential energy as maintained by *external* agencies does not constitute a response; the second, that the liberation of potential energy
as maintained by *internal* agencies does not constitute a
response, either. When both reservations are put together, we must necessarily conclude that the release of
any ordinary potential energy possessed by the living
object does not meet the requirements of the concept. It
thus appears that, biologically speaking, a response represents the liberation of some kind of energy other than
potential. The problem that remains is to specify the kind
of energy actually involved in this liberation.

Response as Release of Chemical Energy. Patently,
the solution to that problem is virtually forced upon us.
If a response is indeed some kind of liberation of energy,
then the energy in question must have been, to begin
with, somehow bound, latent, or—in a broad sense—
potential. It has just been demonstrated that it was not

"potential" in the classical meaning of the term. The sole remaining possibility would seem to be that it was "potential" in the newer and more expanded sense of the word. That is to say, it was energy inherent in chemical bonds and electron orbitals. A *response*, evidently, *is the liberation of chemical energy.*

So much would seem to be transparent. There does remain, however, the material question of whether or not this energy must be released in any specific fashion, to qualify the event as a biological response. We have already narrowed 'transformation of energy' to liberation of energy,' and that in turn to 'liberation of chemical energy.' Should the process be carried still further? Is a response some particular kind of expenditure of chemical energy?

Interestingly enough, the indications are clearly negative. Any event at all in which chemical energy is released, seems to emit heat, or to produce electromagnetic radiation. These basic manifestations may, of course, be cast in such familiar patterns as walking, swimming, flying, spinning a web, biting, emitting electrical shocks, thinking, talking, or illuminating one's abdominal segment from within. As long as the energy released by the living object is that of the formation or disruption of chemical bonds, and not merely that of an object previously held at bay in a field of force, it seems to qualify as a response.

Another question, intriguing if tangential, also arises at this point. Does biology ever regard the *absorption* of chemical energy as a response? It might; but evidently it does not. The mere acceptance of photons by the retina is never called a "response," for example. Nor would a protozoan be said to be responding if it should, for some reason, remain at a level of temperature lower than that of its environment. The process of *turning* cold might, rightly or wrongly, be inferred to be a response; but the simple state of *being* cold, of absorbing thermal energy into chemical structure, would not be so regarded.

Our definition would seem to stand. To the biologist, then, *a response is any liberation of chemical energy by a living object.* This is the definition which will be accepted here, and the one which will provide a foundation for further discussion. Our immediate problem now, in pursuit of that discussion, is to formulate a satisfactory definition for the biological concept of 'stimulus.'

'Stimulus' in Biology

The biologist's definition of 'stimulus' is usually a rather simple one. Typically, it amounts to the plain statement that a stimulus is anything that causes a response. As the biologist himself recognizes, however, the problem is not really that simple. Indeed, there are certain misgivings about the typical definition which are so common as to be almost standard.

In the present essay, we shall accept the unqualified definition of 'stimulus' as 'anything that causes a response'; but we shall accept it only temporarily, regarding it merely as a basal, working formulation, soon to be modified in the light of our examination of the usual reservations. The latter examination will be carried out in two sections, dealing respectively with (1) the stimulus as a causal agent, and (2) stimuli which are under- and overadequate. A final section will concern itself with the ultimate definition of 'stimulus' as a biological term.

The Stimulus as a Cause. To anyone familiar with Verworn's classical *Irritability* (1916), one major misgiving about the basal definition will occur immediately: it seems to fall into the naïve presumption that any such single, isolated agency as a stimulus *can* be "the cause" of a response. Verworn emphasized repeatedly that causation is multiple and holistic; and that the stimulus, often regarded as the cause of a response, is really no more than one of a great many conditions necessary to its occurrence: the one which happens to be the last fulfilled (Verworn 1916: 18ff., e.g.).

Verworn's own pursuit of this line of thought was rather tortuous, and his eventual characterization of the stimulus as *"every change in the vital conditions"* (1916: 31, 35ff.) was not entirely convincing. There is no denying Verworn's basic point, but it would seem to be a point which is not so much forgotten in biological thought as it is taken for granted. It is true enough that the response of a living object to a given stimulus depends not only upon the stimulus itself but upon the entire milieu of the object, as well. It is also true, nevertheless, that the living object's environment works its effect only by changing the object itself, that the milieu is of importance only to the extent that it alters the organism. If the living object is completely specified, the general environment is automatically taken into account. If the living object is completely specified, too, the response elicited by a given stimulus is quite predictable. In this practical sense, a single stimulating event can legitimately be said to cause a response; and our working definition of 'stimulus' as 'anything that causes a response' is therefore not invalid from the outset, at least.

Having established this point, we may still wish to make some concession to the spirit of Verworn's argument. The word 'cause' does indeed, in the context of our definition, invite misinterpretation; and there is much to be said for replacing it with a less forceful alternative. The word 'produce' would seem to be appropriate. In its first revision, then, our basal definition of 'stimulus' would necessarily become 'anything that *produces* a response.' We have now improved the definition; but we have also made it vulnerable to a new misinterpretation.

For 'produce' is an ambiguous word. Is it the sun which "produces" the motor response in the plant—or the sunlight? Does the buzzer "produce" the pinna reflex—or the sound of the buzzer? Here is the question of the distal stimulus versus the proximal stimulus, a question which has on the whole seemed to perturb biologists rather less than psychologists. Biology has traditionally hewn, in this matter, to the line of the proximal stimulus. It has clearly rejected, as stimuli, objects and events remote from the organism itself; and it has refused to exploit terms like 'produce' to stretch the concept of causation beyond all reasonable limits. Thus, although the sun may, in a sense, produce the response in the plant, it does so only with the cooperation of a number of extraneous variables (for example, there must be nothing opaque between the sun and the plant). Accordingly, the sun is not actually causal and not properly a stimulus. The buzzer, too, will produce the pinna reflex only when an acoustic medium lies between it and the ear of the animal in question (to name just one condition). The buzzer itself is therefore not the real stimulus.

Manifestly, we need to dispel the ambiguity introduced into our definition by the use of the word 'produce,' and to make sure we are faithfully representing the biologist's intentions. What is indicated is a revision of our formulation to stress the proximal nature of the stimulus. Such a revision is not difficult to accomplish, and our definition now assumes a new form. 'Stimulus' becomes '*any event, within or upon a living object*, that produces a response.'

Subliminal and Assaultive Stimuli.   In the preceding section, we have weighed one misgiving concerning our basal definition of 'stimulus,' and we have modified and remodified the definition in such a way as to take account of it. We may now move on to consider the second of the common misgivings—one which virtually springs to mind as we read even the revised statement at which we have just arrived.

The issue is simple. Our definition now asserts that a stimulus produces a response. Nothing is more obvious, however, than the fact that many stimuli do *not* produce responses. They may tend to, or they may be intended to; but, in actuality, they remain subliminal and ineffective. It is thus clear that any adequate definition of the word 'stimulus' must accommodate the case of the subthreshold stimulus; and it is interesting that a certain amount of serious thought has already been devoted to the question of how it might do so (cf. Heilbrunn 1952: 564–568).

Altogether, no one seems yet to have brought forth an acceptable answer to the question. This is a somewhat puzzling circumstance, inasmuch as the nature of what is required would seem to be fairly evident. In just a moment, in fact, we shall recast our own definition to recognize the concept of subliminal stimulation. Before we do so, however, it will be convenient to consider briefly one final qualification to be placed upon any delineation of the concept of 'stimulus.'

The point to be raised is this. The definition of 'stimulus' ought to make plain the universal presumption that, although a stimulus may do *less* than initiate a response, it does not do *more* than that. It does not, to any material degree, cut, burn, freeze, maim, or poison. It is merely (as the etymology of the word itself proclaims) a stick, a prod, a goad: an agency calculated to prompt behavior but not to alter the living object by direct action. This stipulation hardly needs to be stressed, and there should really be little argument as to its validity or as to the necessity for recognizing it in the final definition.

We return, then, to the problem of recasting our changing definition of 'stimulus.' It will be recalled that the condition in which we left that definition was this: *A stimulus is any event, within or upon a living object, that produces a response.* We wish now to modify this formulation, with a dual purpose. First, we wish to accommodate the possibility of subliminal stimulation; and second, we wish to specify that the maximal effect of any stimulus is the evocation of a response. Both of these ends would seem to be achieved if we adopted the following restatement of our definition: *A stimulus is any event, within or upon a living object, which has a material effect upon that object only insofar as it produces a response.*

The Biological Definition of 'Stimulus.' It could be successfully argued, I believe, that we have now reached our goal; that, to biology, a stimulus is indeed any event, within or upon a living object, which has a material effect upon that object only insofar as it produces a response. The picture our definition draws is that of some proximal circumstance which may or may not elicit a response; but which, in either case, is presumed to have no collateral effect of any importance to us. This certainly is the picture of a stimulus.

It is a matter of considerable interest that, when we use the word 'stimulus,' we are evidently passing a distinctly subjective judgment as to the "material effects" of the event in question. Any stimulus is bound to have *some* collateral effect, however subtle, upon the living object. There is, after all, no such thing as pure stimulation. It is thus up to the scientific observer to decide for himself whether or not such effects are "material" in terms of the observations he seeks to make. Probably most stimuli involve side effects which are negligible in any case, and the judgment is not difficult. It is possible that side effects which are trivial for some purposes are actually of some importance for others. And it is an intriguing thought that occasionally a major insult to the organism might be viewed legitimately, from a certain specialized standpoint, as a stimulus; thus, we might validly inquire into the effect of atomic radiations as stimuli, quite apart from their ultimate destructive effect upon the organism.

It would appear that the concept of 'stimulus' is itself a complex one and that our definition has merely reflected this complexity.

Summary

We have scrutinized the biological concepts of 'stimulus' and 'response,' partly for their own sakes and partly by way of introduction to the chapter which follows. We have come to the conclusion that the word 'stimulus' means 'any event, within or upon a living object, which has a material effect upon that object only insofar as it produces a response'; and that the word 'response' means 'any liberation of chemical energy by a living object.'

REFERENCES

Bard, P. 1935. In: Macleod, J. J. R.; 1935; *Physiology in Modern Medicine* (seventh edition) ; Mosby, St. Louis.

Best, C. H., and N. B. Taylor. 1950. *The Physiological Basis of Medical Practice* (fifth edition). Williams and Wilkins, Baltimore.

Halliburton, W. D., and R. J. S. McDowall. 1935. *Handbook of Physiology* (thirty-fourth edition). Blakiston, Philadelphia.

Heilbrunn, L. V. 1952. *An Outline of General Physiology* (third edition). Saunders, Philadelphia and London.

Scheer, B. T. 1948. *Comparative Physiology*. Wiley, New York.

Verworn, M. 1916. *Irritability*. Yale University Press, New Haven, Connecticut.

NOTES

The content of the foregoing chapter was summarized in the presidential address to the North Carolina Psychological Association in 1962, and outlined in some detail to the Dartmouth College Psychological Colloquium in the same year. An abstract of the former presentation can be found in *The Journal of the Elisha Mitchell Scientific Society*, 1962, *78*, 107.

III

'STIMULUS' AND 'RESPONSE'
IN PSYCHOLOGY

THE PREVIOUS CHAPTER has examined the concepts associated with the words 'stimulus' and 'response' in the realm of biology. The present chapter will go on, to finish the dual task originally undertaken. It will analyze the notions connected with the same words in the realm of psychology.

It might be said that the need for such an analysis seems to be particularly urgent. In biology, 'stimulus' and 'response' are important terms. In psychology, they are central. To the extent that psychology is confused about their meaning, it is confused about its own task and condition; and it would appear that, in fact, the terms are now but vaguely realized.

In pursuing its own examination of the concepts of 'stimulus' and 'response,' the present essay builds directly upon the two which have preceded it. It thus adopts a basic viewpoint which is physicalistic, reductionistic, and deterministic; it commits itself strictly to physical monism as an explanation of conscious experience; and it utilizes the definitions of the biological concepts of 'stimulus' and 'response' which were developed earlier: *A stimulus is any event, within or upon a living object, which has a material effect upon that object only insofar as it produces a response;* and *a response is any liberation of chemical energy by a living object.* Upon these bases, it now proceeds.

Although the science of biology tends, as we have seen, to be somewhat inarticulate on the topics of stimulus and response, its pronouncements, when they do come, have about them a certain consistency and logic. We can thus speak with reasonable assurance about what "the biologist" says or might say. Unfortunately, the situation in psychology is not nearly so simple. We find here an almost bewildering diversity of statement, along with a real penchant for definitions which are circular either in fact or in appearance. In the face of such confusion, it is difficult to settle upon a plan to be followed in analyzing the psychological concepts of 'stimulus' and 'response.' Everything considered, however, it seems best to pursue essentially the same course as was followed in scrutinizing the corresponding biological concepts. Thus, we shall attempt to deal first with the notion of 'response' and then with that of 'stimulus.' A brief, final section will explore the significance of the conclusions reached in the body of the paper.

'Response' in Psychology

The examination of the psychological concept of 'response' will be divided into three parts. The first part will consist of a brief historical review, made advisable by the diversity of statement already mentioned. The second part will deal with, and dispose of, the possibility of logical circularity in the customary definitions of 'response.' The third part will attempt to abstract from the material reviewed the essential idea represented by the term in question.

Historical Sketch. In the history of psychology, 'response' made a somewhat belated appearance. 'Stimulus' found use from the first; for the German psychophysicists, generally regarded as the founders of scientific psychology, were greatly concerned with the external agencies which gave rise to conscious experience. The psychophysicists were not, on the other hand, interested in the overt reactions of their observers; hence, no terminological problem arose in this area.

When 'response' finally did appear, it was with the air of having drifted casually into psychology from biology. The word began to be used widely by the early American psychologists, who were self-consciously biological in their systematic orientation, in the evident conviction that they were employing a recognized biological term in an established fashion. Completely typical was the treatment 'response' received from William James: he introduced the word in the opening pages of his *Principles* (James 1896: 12), used it freely throughout the book, but bothered neither to define it nor to list it in his index.

When J. B. Watson launched "Behaviorism," he was, as is well known, urging upon the world a veritable science of stimulus and response. Accepting full responsibility for his own basic terms, Watson formulated rather lengthy characterizations of them. These characterizations now serve quite well to summarize and elucidate the meanings that had already accrued to the words, inasmuch as Watson's use of the terms was essentially like that of his predecessors. His definitions are also of particular interest because, to an appreciable extent, they became the norms which were to prevail through the years that followed. In the light of these facts, the present paper will pay fairly close attention to Watson's treatment of both 'stimulus' and 'response.'

Of especial importance at the moment, of course, is his notion of 'response.' It is stated explicitly in *Psychology from the Standpoint of a Behaviorist,* and two passages from that volume will typify Watson's position:

. . . we employ in psychology the physiological term
"response," but . . . we must slightly extend its use.
The movements which result from a tap on the patellar
tendon, or from stroking the soles of the feet are "simple" responses which are studied both in physiology
and in medicine. In psychology our study, too, is sometimes concerned with simple responses of these types,
but more often with several complex responses taking
place simultaneously. In the latter case we sometimes
use the popular term "act" or adjustment, meaning by
that that the whole group of responses is integrated in
such a way (instinct or habit) that the individual does
something which we have a name for, that is, "takes
food," "builds a house," "swims," "writes a letter,"
"talks.". . . But it should be well understood that
whatever the man does under stimulation is a response
or adjustment—blushing, increased heartbeat, change
in respiration, etc., are definite part adjustments. . . .
Usually when we speak of response we mean that the
organism goes forward to right or left, or retracts as a
whole, that it eats, drinks, fights, builds houses, or
engages in trade. But these patent and easily observa-
ble changes do not exhaust the term 'response.'. . .
We should mean by response the total striped and un-
striped muscular and glandular changes which follow
upon a given stimulus. [Watson 1924: 11–14]

. . . a good many psychologists have misunderstood the
behaviorist's position. They insist that he is only ob-
serving the individual movements of the muscles and
glands; that he is interested in the muscles and glands
in exactly the same way the physiologist is interested
in them. This is not the whole statement. *The behaviorist is interested in integrations and total activities of
the individual.* . . . In the occupations and activities of
individuals we do not stop as a rule to reduce the total
activity to muscle twitches. We can do it if necessary
and we do do it at times. . . . In the psychological
laboratory we do find it necessary often to study the

details of the total activity we see in daily life. [Watson
1924: 39–41]

There is much deserving of comment in this delineation.
It will be recalled, however, that our business at the
moment is that of prosecuting a brief historical review.
Accordingly, comment will be reserved for later sections.

Among the most Watsonian of Watson's successors
was C. L. Hull; and, in his "Primary Principle of Stimulation," we find him reemphasizing the biological orientation typical of Watson himself:

> . . . a small amount of energy acting on some special-
> ized structure will release . . . energy from some other
> source. . . . A familiar example is the trigger action of
> a gun. . . . The principle of stimulation is operative at
> several points in the integrative apparatus of the mam-
> malian organism. [Hull 1943: 39]

It is of interest, however, that Hull's biological stress,
like Watson's, was accompanied by an even greater
stress upon the larger units of behavior. Hull refers repeatedly and with force to "adaptive behavior," "organismic behavior," and "molar behavior" (Hull 1943: 18,
19, 28, 31). Organisms are said to "do something" and to
"act" (Hull 1943: 50). In this respect, Hull is rather
surprisingly in accord with E. C. Tolman. The latter,
surely the *least* Watsonian of Watson's successors, contended vigorously that the sort of behavior in which the
psychologist is really interested is necessarily "molar,"
necessarily prompted by the organism's "expectations."
For Tolman, for example, stimuli were simply "environmental entities which evoke expectations" (Tolman
1932; 1ff.; 454).

Between the extremes of "muscle twitches" and "expectations," there has always lain a middle course. Thus,
in 1933, Kantor gave expression to the following view:

Stimuli and responses are reciprocal factors in a behavior segment. One cannot occur without the other. Probably the best way to describe a response is to say that it is something that the organism does with respect to the stimulus object. *The organism performs some action or movement.* The stimulus, on the other hand, is an action or an operation performed upon the organism by the object with which it interacts. This stimulus action can best be defined as the evocation or the incitement of an action on the part of the organism. [Kantor 1933: 21–22; italics added]

In this vein, too, we find Skinner's classical treatment:

Behavior is what an organism is *doing* . . . that part of the functioning of an organism which is engaged in acting upon or having commerce with the outside world . . . the movement of an organism or of its parts in a frame of reference. [Skinner 1938: 6] . . . But . . . The environment enters into a description of behavior when it can be shown that a given *part* of behavior may be induced at will (or according to certain laws) by a modification in part of the forces affecting the organism. Such a part, or modification of a part, of the environment is traditionally called a *stimulus* and the correlated part of the behavior a *response*. Neither term may be defined as to its essential properties without the other. [Skinner 1938: 9]

Skinner's view is brought into especially sharp focus by Keller and Schoenfeld's more recent volume. Here the statement is as follows:

Through analysis, psychologists have arrived at the concepts of *stimulus* and *response*. A stimulus may be provisionally defined as "a part, or change in a part, of the environment," and a response may be defined as "a part, or a change in a part, of behavior." We shall recognize, however, that a *stimulus* cannot be defined independently of a response. An environmental event becomes a stimulus by virtue of the fact that it is followed by a response. [Keller and Schoenfeld 1950: 3]

Again, this sort of formulation invites comment; and again, we remind ourselves that our present concern is purely historical.

In point of fact, however, this concern with history is one which is about to end. The citations already set forth do not misrepresent either the range or the median of customary psychological thought. In general, there would be small profit in adding to them. Before closing entirely, though, we should recognize a viewpoint which seems almost to lie on a new continuum. It is that of N. E. Miller:

> . . . a response is any activity by or within the individual which can become functionally connected with an antecedent event through learning; a stimulus is any event to which a response can be so connected. [Miller 1959: 239]

Miller's formulation will turn out to have a special value for us in the end and to be more like the orthodox definitions than one might at first suppose.

Our brief historical review thus does come to a close. Our eventual problem will, of course, be that of abstracting from the definitions cited some reasonable concept of "response." Our immediate problem, however, is one of formal logical analysis, and that is the matter we turn to next.

Circularity in the Definition of 'Response.' It was mentioned to begin with that the psychological definitions of 'stimulus' and 'response' tend to be characterized by the superficial appearance, or even the actual incidence, of logical circularity: there seems to be a strong inclination to specify each word in terms of the other. That inclination occasionally finds complete expression, as in one definition not already mentioned:

> All those actions of the environment which produce
> reactions or adjustments of the body are summed up
> under the term *stimulus;* and the terms adjustment
> and reaction indicate the effects of stimuli. [Dunlap
> 1928 : 22]

At other times, circularity is not immediately apparent;
but one is still left with the strong suspicion that it is
indeed present and that the formulation in question is
actually useless.

Now, at least some of the definitions mentioned in the
historical sketch above present real problems in this
connection. The formulations of Kantor and Skinner, for
example, raise obvious questions. Some of the same questions are also involved, albeit in a more attenuated form,
in Watson's characterization. It will thus be necessary to
examine the definitions above from the standpoint of the
issue of circularity; and we shall do so now, taking them
in their order of original presentation.

First, then, as to Watson's version. Here, the threat of
circularity arises from Watson's frequent use of the
word 'stimulus' in his delineation of 'response.' As one
might suspect, and as we shall shortly confirm, Watson
also used 'response' (or its synonyms) in his definition
of 'stimulus.' He thus put himself in distinct peril of
defining each word in terms of the other, and therefore of
ultimately defining neither one at all. In the end, however, Watson's characterizations are not seriously compromised. Specifically, and to the point at hand, the word
'stimulus' does not figure *crucially* in his definition of
'response.' It is there; but it appears to creep in, not
of any logical necessity, but merely as an expression of
Watson's faith that every response has its stimulus. The
characterization of psychological responses as "simple
biological responses . . . 'acts' or adjustments . . . doing
something we have a name for . . . integrations and
total activities of the individual," still stands quite inde-

pendently of the term 'stimulus.' It is well for Watson
that it does, incidentally, because his definition of 'stimulus' *does* truly depend on the idea of 'response.' For
the moment, however, we content ourselves with the observation that Watson's delineation of 'response' itself
is logically acceptable.

What Watson could have done, both Hull and Tolman
actually did do. Thus, although both of the latter men
strongly emphasized "molar behavior," as did Watson,
neither made Watson's error of invoking, even superfi-
cially, the notion of 'stimulus' in the definition of 'response.' The formulations of Tolman and Hull accordingly stir no suspicion of circularity. When we move on
to the statements of Kantor, Skinner, and Keller and
Schoenfeld, on the other hand, our misgivings become
acute; for all of these writers seem to insist, deliberately,
upon defining 'stimulus' in terms of 'response,' and
vice versa. Patently, theirs is a position we should examine closely.

As it happens, close examination is repaid in this instance by an intriguing discovery: appearances and the
seeming contentions of the authors to the contrary, the
definitions proposed by Kantor, Skinner, and Keller and
Schoenfeld actually present no problem of circularity
whatsoever. To satisfy ourselves as to the validity of this
statement, we need only note that all of these men share a
definite concept of 'response' *as an abstract category,*
and that the verbalization of this concept is not at all
contaminated by any dependence upon 'stimulus.' In
Kantor's view, for instance, "The organism performs
some action or movement"; for Skinner, "Behavior is
what an organism is *doing* . . . acting upon or having
commerce with the outside world"; and, to Keller and
Schoenfeld, "a response is a part of behavior." These
writers are, in short, proposing quite the same definition
for 'response' as are Watson, Tolman, and Hull; and

there is nothing at all circular about it. True enough, they are also urging another point—namely, that the identification of the stimulus eliciting any *particular* response ought to enter into the specification of that response; and, true enough, their advocacy of this point gives their statements a misleading cast of circularity. Within the framework of our own immediate concern, however, it is plain that Kantor, Skinner, and Keller and Schoenfeld have provided logically defensible characterizations.

The same can be said, in fine, for Miller's somewhat unique definition. Miller himself expresses a real concern with the problem of logical circularity (Miller 1959: 239ff.). At least in terms of our own momentary interest, however, his limning of 'response' is irreproachable: "a response is any activity . . . which can become functionally connected with an antecedent event through learning." This definition depends crucially upon the notion of 'learning,' itself an elusive concept; but the definition is not, in any case, a circular one.

The Psychological Concept of 'Response.' It has now become patent that the usual psychological definitions of 'response' are, in fact, formally acceptable. The question that remains to be answered, then, is that of the substance of these definitions: what do they really mean?

A review of our list of samples, conducted with this question in mind, will actually discover a very considerable area of agreement. For one thing, it is clear that the psychological response is universally regarded as a particular variety of the biological: it is an instance of the liberation of chemical energy by a living object. For another thing, there is emphatic agreement that, on the other hand, the psychological response is not just *any* kind of biological response: it has some property which is unique, and which is obviously crucial to valid definition.

The nature of this property we find rendered in a number of rather different ways. Thus, the psychological response is described as an "act," an "adjustment," "something we have a name for," a "total muscular and glandular change," an "integration," "total activity," "adaptive behavior," "organic behavior," "molar behavior," "what an organism is doing," or a "response of the whole organism." Clearly, we must decide what these various renditions can mean.

In attempting to make this decision, we are forced immediately to the plain truth that, taken literally, these phrases are actually quite meaningless. They are thoroughly familiar to the psychologist, and, over the years, he has come to accept or tolerate them. The fact remains, however, that they are clearly of no value whatsoever in distinguishing psychological responses from other biological responses. It is obvious that any biological response at all can be regarded as an "act," or an "adjustment," or "something we have a name for"—and so on down the list. And it does no good to say that psychology deals with "total activities" or "responses of the whole organism," because it simply does not.

If, then, these terms cannot be taken literally, we are obliged to take them figuratively. We must regard them as symbolic of some criterion which the psychologist is unable or unwilling to put into words. It is not difficult to surmise what this criterion is, for "the behaviorists . . . solve their problem by using language in a specialized way, namely by refusing to use at all such words as . . . 'conscious' " (Bridgman 1959: vi). Behind the circumlocutions of "response of the whole organism," "molar behavior," "total activity," "adjustment," and the like, lies the simple meaning: a psychological response is a biological response of the particular sort which is contingent upon conscious experience—not necessarily upon deliberate or memorable thought, of course; but certainly upon the bare, primitive fact of awareness; typically, upon sensation.

It is true that this conclusion rests in considerable part upon the cryptic nature of the usual psychological definitions of 'response' and the evident impossibility of understanding them on any basis other than the one suggested. The conclusion is also strongly supported, however, by the words of Miller's rather unorthodox definition, cited earlier ("a response is any activity . . . which can become functionally connected with an antecedent event through learning"). Avoiding for the moment any scrutiny of the notion of 'learning,' we need only note that Miller has, in his definition, simply described the classical psychological technique for establishing the presence of conscious processes in a lower (or higher) animal. Traditionally, any cue to which a biological response can be connected by learning is a cue which is assumed to evoke consciousness. When, therefore, Miller restricts his category of 'psychological response' to those biological responses which can be attached to cues, he is almost explicitly concurring in the definition here abstracted from the more customary statements.

He who would rebut the definition at which we have arrived is likely to recall a fact over which we have so far skipped rather lightly, but one which, in the end, reinforces rather than damages the formulation. The fact in question is this: several of the definitions of 'response' which were cited above as typical made specific reference to "simple response," "muscle twitches," or "movements," and indicated that the psychologist is properly concerned with even these primitive biological responses. This attitude would seem to imply that psychological responses are not always instigated by conscious experience and, consequently, that our own definition is not entirely valid. It will be remembered, however, that there was an air of reservation about the way in which these simple responses were acknowledged as psychological; even Watson gave them but a grudging admittance. The reservation, of course, is precisely that even *these* responses must be contingent upon conscious experience. The psychologist is not interested, as a psychologist, in even such complex behavior as digestion, heartbeat, vascular contraction, or reflexive somatic response as it normally goes on; when this kind of behavior becomes sensitive to conscious experience, the psychologist becomes interested—but not before. What psychologist would do research on peristaltic contraction in the intestine of the anesthetized dog? What psychological journal would publish a paper on the strength of the patellar reflex as a function of the force with which the tendon is struck?

We may now, perhaps, bring the argument to a close. We shall take it that *a psychological response is the particular sort of biological response which is contingent upon, aroused by, conscious experience*. A completely explicit definition would, of course, describe it as *any liberation of chemical energy by a living object, as produced by conscious experience*.

We shall turn now to the delineation of the psychological concept of 'stimulus,' a task somewhat simpler than the one we have just completed.

'Stimulus' in Psychology

In examining the psychological notion of 'stimulus,' we shall find it convenient to follow the same general plan we followed in analyzing the corresponding concept in biology. In the present section, a brief historical review seems advisable (see Herman 1957 and Gibson 1960 for additional historical material); but we shall terminate that review by stating, as was done for the biological concept, a basal definition of 'stimulus.' We shall then go on to consider the issues of proximal and distal, and of subliminal and disruptive, stimuli. Finally, we shall conclude by attempting to provide an exact formulation of the concept.

Historical Sketch. We have already noted that 'stimulus' appeared with the very founding of psychology. To the psychophysicist, *der Reiz* (stimulus) was the external agency that prompted the conscious experience he wished to analyze and measure. When psychophysics moved to America with E. B. Titchener, *'der Reiz'* moved too. Now as 'the stimulus,' it appeared time and again in Titchener's writings. It was seldom defined, but its meaning was clear: "The object or process which gives rise to a sensation is termed the *stimulus* to that sensation" (Titchener 1912: 40).

But Titchener was not the only American psychologist of his day, and not all of the others were Titchenerians. As a general thing, then, 'stimulus' drifted into American psychology (just as 'response' did) from the realm of biology. Once more, the early writers were content to use a biological term with little or no formal elucidation. Once more, for example, James's *Principles* introduced a word early (James 1896: 12), used it continually, and did not trouble to define it or to carry it in the index. And once more we turn to J. B. Watson for a delineation which summarized psychological thinking before its time, and anticipated that which was to follow.

In company with Watson's definition of 'response,' already quoted above from *Psychology from the Standpoint of a Behaviorist*, we find his characterization of 'stimulus':

We use the term *stimulus* in psychology as it is used in physiology. Only in psychology we have to extend somewhat the usage of the term. In the psychological labora-

tory, when we are dealing with relatively simple factors . . . and are attempting to isolate their effects
upon the adjustments of men, we speak of stimuli. On
the other hand, when the factors leading to reactions
are more complex, as, for example, in the social world,
we speak of *situations*. A situation is, of course, upon
final analysis, resolvable into a complex group of stimuli. As examples of stimuli we may name such things as
rays of light . . . sound waves . . . gaseous particles
[that] affect the membrane of the nose . . . solutions
[which act upon] the taste buds . . . solid objects
which affect the skin and mucous membrane . . . ra-
diant stimuli . . . noxious stimuli. Finally, movements
of the muscles and activity in the glands themselves
serve as stimuli by acting upon the afferent nerve endings in the moving muscles. . . . It is convenient to
speak of a total mass of stimulating factors, which lead
man to react as a whole, as a situation. Situations can
be of the simplest kind or of the greatest complexity. It
should be noted here, finally that there are many forms
of physical energy which do not directly affect our
sense organs. As examples we may cite the facts that
ether waves longer than $760\mu\mu$ [*sic*] or shorter than
$397\mu\mu$ do not lead to visual reactions, and that many of
the wave motions in the air are of such length or
amplitude that they do not produce auditory stimulation. [Watson 1924: 10–11]

It will be recalled that two of Watson's most influen-
cial successors were Hull and Tolman, and we have already seen something of their respective ideas of 'stimulus' in connection with their treatments of 'response.'
Thus, we find Hull pointing out that "a small amount of
energy acting on some specialized structure will release
. . . energy from some other source. . . . A familiar
example is the trigger action of a gun. . . . The principle
of stimulation is operative at several points in the inte-
grative apparatus of the mammalian organism" (Hull

1943: 39); and Tolman conceptualizing stimuli in quite different terms, as "environmental entities which evoke expectations: i.e., sign-gestalt-perceptions -mnemonizations or -inferences" (Tolman 1932: 454). The chasm which appears to separate these two men is not, however, quite so immense as one might think, the situation in respect of their positions on 'response' thus being replicated here in the case of 'stimulus.' If we read Hull's detailed treatment of stimulation, we find an immediate and pervasive dependence upon "afferent neural impulses"; and liberal allusion to the "responsive receptor," the "sense organ," and the "afferent nerve fiber"; indeed, Hull discusses even "The Reception of Movement" and "The Reception of Spatial Relationships," thus arriving at a point not too far from "sign-gestalt-perception" (Hull 1943: 32–39).

In the earlier consideration of the ways in which Kantor, Skinner, and Keller and Schoenfeld conceptualize 'response,' too, we found it necessary to pay some attention to the ways in which they define 'stimulus.' If we now look back at their formulations, we find virtual unanimity in their treatment of this latter concept:

> This stimulus action can best be defined as the evocation or the incitement of an action on the part of the organism. [Kantor]

> The environment enters into a description of behavior when it can be shown that a given *part* of behavior may be induced at will . . . by a modification in part of the forces affecting the organism. Such a part, or modification of a part, of the environment is traditionally called a *stimulus* and the correlated part of behavior a *response*. Neither term may be defined as to its essential properties without the other. [Skinner]

> A stimulus may be provisionally defined as "a part, or change in a part, of the environment.". . . An environ-

mental event becomes a stimulus by virtue of the fact that it is followed by a response. [Keller and Schoenfeld]

We see here rather clearly the lineaments of a concept of 'stimulus' as 'something that evokes a response'; and this is a concept to which Watson and Hull (if not Tolman) could also readily subscribe. Miller, it will be recalled, took a substantially different approach to 'stimulus' as well as to 'response.' His version was this: ". . . a stimulus is any event to which a response can be . . . connected through learning." We shall discover eventually that, once again, Miller's words will have a special value in illuminating a difficult concept.

At this point, our historical sketch comes to an end. Our task now is that of abstracting from it at least a first approximation to the definition we seek. Undoubtedly, there are several ways of going about this task, but the one I should like to follow here involves a convenient simplification: for the time being, I should like to concentrate upon what might be called the orthodox behaviorist's concept of 'stimulus.' Thus, not only Titchener, but Tolman and Miller, as well, are to be set aside for the moment, with the promise that we shall return to them later. Our attention is focused temporarily, then, upon Watson, Kantor, Hull, Skinner and others of their persuasion.

Granted this convenient limitation of scope, we can easily find an adequate working definition of 'stimulus' in the characterization already suggested just above: "a stimulus is something that evokes a response." Formally, this statement so closely resembles the biologist's basic definition that it might as well be rendered in the same terms. Thus, for the psychologist as for the biologist, a stimulus is essentially *anything that produces a response.*

But here we must be careful. We need to keep in mind that, while the 'response' in the biologist's definition is the *biological* 'response,' the 'response' in the psychologist's definition is strictly *psychological*. Hence, when the psychologist defines 'stimulus' as 'anything that produces a response,' he is in reality defining it as "anything that produces a biological response via conscious experience"; and it is plain that this latter specification reduces readily, at least at the level of precision upon which we are now working, to a simpler one: 'anything that produces conscious experience.'

These words come strangely from behavioristic lips— from Watson, Kantor, Hull, and Skinner! All the same, they plainly constitute the formulation which lies implicit within the behaviorist's own verbal habits. It is a formulation that might even have been anticipated from the beginning. We need only recall Watson's classical characterization of the stimulus. In that characterization, there is, of course, a strong primary emphasis upon stimuli as "factors leading to reactions" or as "factors which lead man to react as whole." All the same, Watson is careful to remind us that:

> . . . there are many forms of physical energy which do not directly affect our sense organs. As examples we may cite the facts that ether waves longer than $760\mu\mu$ or shorter than $397\mu\mu$ do not lead to visual reactions, and that many of the wave motions in the air are of such length or amplitude that they do not produce auditory stimulation.

Remembering that these words were set down in a day when the arousal of sensation was the customary indicium of whether an agency did or did not "affect our sense organs," "lead to visual reactions," or "produce auditory stimulation," we realize that even Watson had not forsworn the notion of stimuli as instigators of conscious experience.

To the extent that the definition we have extracted from behavioristic usage seems to defy its own heritage, it must, of course, fall in with the opposing tradition. Clearly it does. It is essentially synonymous with Titchener's own formulation, as cited earlier; and it would never offend Tolmanian phenomenology. Apparently, behaviorism has not been quite so radical, at least in regard to the present issue, as it has often been thought to be.

The essential identity of viewpoint, as between behaviorist and nonbehaviorist, can be given final and rather striking demonstration by the characterization already quoted from N. E. Miller: "a stimulus is any event to which a response can be . . . connected through learning." Miller is widely known as a behavioristic theorist, and the definition with which he presents us here clearly reflects his orientation. At the same time, it is a definition which lends itself to precisely the kind of interpretation we have already applied to Miller's characterization of 'response': to say that a response can be connected by learning with a given cue is traditionally to say that the latter gives rise to conscious experience. Miller's neobehavioristic definition of 'stimulus' is thus seen to be (like the more orthodox, paleobehavioristic definition already explicated) completely identical with the nonbehavioristic formulation.

Now, we have, of course, broken the confines of our original, simplifying restriction. The typification of 'stimulus' as 'anything that produces conscious experience' is palpably valid not only within behaviorism, but for psychology at large. Such a formulation is, however, still a somewhat primitive one—a "basal definition." The analogous biological definition of 'stimulus' as 'anything that produces a response' was considerably modified in the light of certain misgivings generally held about it. In the same way, the psychological definition at which we have now arrived must be altered somewhat to accommodate valid reservations which arise in its connection. These reservations, it is interesting to note, are precisely those which arose in the case of the biological definition. Thus, they revolve about the issues of the distal and the proximal, and the underadequate and the overadequate, stimulus. We shall now turn to these issues, attempting to resolve them and seeking to revise our basic definition of 'stimulus' in terms of the conclusions to which we seem to be led.

The Distal Stimulus and the Proximal Stimulus. It will be recalled that the question of the distal concept of the stimulus versus the proximal concept was, in biology, scarcely viable; there seemed to be a unanimous consensus in favor of the latter notion. In psychology, the situation is almost, but not quite, the same.

Under pressure to speak rigorously, the psychologist generally does describe the stimulus as a proximal event. In 1924, as we have seen, Watson listed the following examples of stimuli: ". . . rays of light . . . sound waves . . . gaseous particles [that] affect the membrane of the nose . . . solutions [which act upon] the taste buds . . . movements in the muscles [which] serve as stimuli by acting upon the afferent nerve endings in the moving muscles." Later, Kantor's definition specified that "The stimulus . . . is an action or an operation performed upon the organism." And Skinner referred to the stimulus as ". . . part of the forces affecting the organism."

When he speaks more casually, however, the psychologist tends toward a distal notion of the stimulus. He begins to refer less to forces impinging directly upon the organism and more to relatively remote features of the environment. A new passage from Watson, actually a somewhat offhand statement made in 1930, will illustrate this tendency:

By stimulus we mean any object in the general environment or any change in the tissues themselves due to the physiological condition of the animal. [Watson 1930: 6]

Similarly, Skinner's definition goes straight on, from the passage cited in the previous paragraph, to say:

Such a part, or modification of a part, of the environment is traditionally called a *stimulus*. . . .

And Keller and Schoenfeld echo this latter formulation in their own definition of the 'stimulus' as 'a part, or a change in a part, of the environment.'

Psychologists recognize their own lack of rigor in speaking of the stimulus as a distal, environmental entity; but they are inclined to justify the practice in terms of convenience in discourse. It is not uncommon, for example, to find such a definition accompanied by an apologetic statement to the effect that the *real* stimuli are, of course, the forces acting directly upon the organism, and that a formulation in terms of environmental objects is merely a matter of verbal simplification. Frequently, this sort of hypocrisy is avoided by making an explicit differentiation between the "true stimulus," on one hand, and the "stimulus object" or "stimulus situation," on the other (cf. Gibson 1960). Such a differentiation is honored in the passage originally quoted from Kantor, for instance; and it is also stressed by Hull (Hull 1943: 32–33). Altogether, it is clear that any definition of 'stimulus' which departs from the fundamental concept of an event 'within or upon' the living object is generally viewed as an unfortunate blurring of systematic distinctions (cf. English and English 1958: 524–525). Almost the only practitioners who are inclined toward a deliberately distal definition of the stimulus are those of phenomenological bent, for whom, in any case, the blurring of distinctions often seems to constitute a doctrinal virtue (cf. Tolman 1932: 454; Gibson 1960).

The upshot of this discussion is the conclusion that the stimulus is a proximal event, to the psychologist as to the biologist. Everything considered, it would seem wise to strengthen our working definition of 'stimulus' by making that point clear; and there is no reason why we should not do so in the same terms we employed in affecting the analogous change in our biological definition. The process of revision is thus simple. Our current definition is this: 'Stimulus' means 'anything that produces conscious experience.' Appropriately recast, that definition would become: *'Stimulus'* means *'any event, within or upon a living object, which produces conscious experience.'* Let us consider the revision as made, and the latter statement as our new working characterization of "stimulus."

Subliminal and Disruptive Stimuli. We now have as our single remaining task still another one which also had to be performed for the biological definition of 'stimulus.' We need to modify our present formulation to take account of the possibility of subliminal stimulation; at the same time, we need to provide explicitly against any side effects the stimulus may produce.

The situation in psychology at large with respect to the notion of subthreshold stimulation is indeed a curious one. Side by side, we find the two completely contradictory contentions that: (1) a stimulus is necessarily effective, and (2) many stimuli are not effective. This bifurcated mode of thought goes back at least as far as Watson; for along with Watson's general insistence that a stimulus is an event which elicits a response goes his warning:

> . . . any stimulus in any sense field can be made so weak that the work it does upon the sense organ is not sufficient to produce . . . a . . . response. [Watson 1924: 52]

In recent years, the contradiction has become even more explicit. Keller and Schoenfeld provide a particularly striking instance:

> An environmental event becomes a stimulus by virtue of the fact that it is followed by a response . . . [but] . . . *a stimulus must be of a certain intensity before it can elicit a response.* [Keller and Schoenfeld 1950: 3, 8]

In their own treatment, however, Keller and Schoenfeld have largely followed Skinner. Thus, we may recall the latter's insistence on the one-to-one relationship between stimulus and response, and contrast that insistence with his "Law of Threshold":

> *The intensity of the stimulus must reach or exceed a certain critical value (called the threshold) in order to elicit a response.* [Skinner 1938: 12]

In fairness, we must emphasize that Skinner, and Keller and Schoenfeld, are far from being isolated in their self-contradiction. One highly respected textbook, for instance, gives repeated prominence to the contention that stimuli are always and necessarily followed by responses (Boring, Langfeld, and Weld 1948: 16, 20, 215, 251), only to dissolve into final confession:

> All living organisms exhibit the phenomena known as *thresholds*. Some stimuli affect them; others do not. [Boring, Langfeld, and Weld 1948: 263]

Another well-known text covers the same sort of retreat much more ingeniously:

> A stimulus is any event inside or outside the organism to which the organism is capable of responding . . . [but] . . . we can not perceive events that are below a certain energy level when they reach the sense organ. Such stimuli (*we may call them stimuli, since they are*

able to stimulate some organisms) are below a minimum needed intensity level. [Brown and Gilhousen 1950: 2, 266; italics added]

Faced by this kind of confusion, the authors of a standard psychological dictionary can only murmur feeble remonstrance:

A physical event impinging on a receptor but not initiating its normal receptor function is often, but improperly, called a stimulus. [English and English 1958: 525]

As a matter of fact, it is difficult to understand what could possibly be "improper" about the concept or the term 'subthreshold stimulus.' It is a useful notion—employed constantly, and endorsed (as we have seen) even by those who oppose it. Thus, our way at this point is clear: we must modify our definition to provide for the case of the stimulus which does not, in fact, arouse a response. Once more, too, we can accomplish this revision in such a way as to provide for the final, and almost trivial, reservation: the one concerning the lack of any substantial side effects consequent upon stimulation. In this fashion, and still following the pathway we established in pursuing the biological concept, we come to a final statement of the psychological notion of 'stimulus': *A stimulus is any event, within or upon a living object, which has a material effect upon that object only insofar as it produces conscious experience.*

The Psychological Definition of 'Stimulus.' There is little left to say about the definition at which we have now arrived. It is, of course, interesting that, commencing with an avowedly behavioristic notion of 'stimulus,' we should end up with the traditional picture of the stimulus as the source of sensation. True enough, this picture has been modified to emphasize the proximal nature of the stimulus and to allow for the possibility of subliminal activation; but the rationale of these modifications has been set forth in terms of general psychological practice, and they seem clearly to be justified. The psychological stimulus emerges as an agency which, working upon the living object, may or may not produce a sensation; but which, in any case, is important only because of whatever sensation it does arouse. As we did in the case of the biological stimulus, we face here the somewhat relativistic question of which collateral effects are or are not "important" or "material"; however, we could do no more here than to repeat the arguments advanced before, and such a procedure scarcely seems profitable.

It has become plain that the psychological concepts of 'stimulus' and 'response' differ considerably from their biological counterparts. In the light of that fact, it now seems desirable to explore in a somewhat formal manner the relationships between those two sets of ideas. The section of the present essay which follows just below will attempt such an exploration.

'Stimulus' and 'Response' in Biology and Psychology

Let us begin by taking note of an obvious relationship —namely, the one between the biological and the psychological ideas of 'response.' It will be recalled that the biological notion of 'response' is that of any liberation of chemical energy by a living object. It will be recalled, too, that the psychological concept is that of any such liberation of energy *as prompted by conscious experience.* It is clear, then, that the psychological response is one species of the biological. A biological response may or may not be a psychological response, but a psychological response is necessarily a biological response; and this relationship is true by definition.

Unhappily, the connection between the biological and psychological concepts of 'stimulus' is not nearly so straightforward. To the biologist, a stimulus is any event, within or upon a living object, which has a material effect upon the object only insofar as it produces a liberation of chemical energy. To the psychologist, a stimulus is any event, within or upon a living object, which has a material effect upon the object only insofar as it evokes *conscious experience*. If conscious experience is itself an instance of the liberation of chemical energy, or if that experience can be aroused only by the prior release of such energy, then the psychological stimulus is indeed a special case of the biological. If the process of consciousness does not meet one of these requirements, then the two kinds of stimulus are actually quite disparate. There is no inevitable logical relationship here, as there was in the case of the concepts of 'response.' The question of whether or not a psychological stimulus is also necessarily a biological stimulus can be answered only by an empirical investigation into the character of consciousness as a physical event. That such an investigation would be a formidable task is immediately obvious; that it would be a truly overwhelming one becomes apparent as we reflect that the nature of conscious experience no doubt differs considerably from organism to organism, and that the mechanism of its arousal certainly varies almost infinitely from one particular instance to another.

There are at least two courses available to one who wishes to rationalize an intuitive conviction that the psychologist's stimulus is indeed a particular variety of the biologist's stimulus. The first is tortuously legalistic, and I describe it here without sponsorship and principally as a matter of incidental interest. The second requires for its pursuit what amounts to an act of scientific faith, but it is one very commonly followed. Each will be considered now, briefly.

It can be contended (to begin with the first sort of argument) that a psychological stimulus, even when it evokes a process of awareness, remains of no material consequence unless the process of awareness, in turn, evokes some sort of further response. A conscious experience which leads neither to perception nor to overt action, and which fails to lend itself to later recollection, could thus be considered negligible in the economy of the organism. A variant of the same argument might be one to the effect that conscious experience, once it happens, always prompts *some* response. One might even choose to believe that the experience of awareness is literally dependent upon the occurrence of a subsequent response (cf. Langfeld 1931). In any case, however, the sort of view exemplified here really comes down to the proposition that a psychological stimulus of any consequence necessarily evokes an efferent biological response, and that the psychological stimulus therefore qualifies perforce as a biological stimulus, too. I think it is clear that this stand is precarious at best.

The second way in which one may rationalize the intuitive conviction that the psychological stimulus is a subclass within the biological category is, as suggested above, the one more usually followed. Thus, it is widely supposed both that (1) the events which lead from stimulation to conscious awareness are themselves biological responses, and that (2) the process of awareness *per se* also represents fundamentally a liberation of chemical energy and is therefore inherently a biological response. Inasmuch as there seems to be a certain amount of information supporting this view, it is not an unreasonable one; and, if it is correct, it certainly solves the problem of the relation between the psychological and biological concepts of 'stimulus.' The latter does then indeed contain the former.

The truth of this matter is, of course, a thing of great interest. We should naturally like to know whether or not the psychological stimulus is in fact a special case of the biological. Apparently, however, the question cannot yet be answered with great confidence, and we shall have to leave the matter at that. Meanwhile, it is of some importance, as will develop during the course of the final chapter of this volume, that biologists and psychologists do at least *think* not only that the psychological response is a species of the biological, but also that the psychological stimulus is a particular instance of the biological stimulus.

Summary

Having scrutinized the biological concepts of 'stimulus' and 'response' in the previous chapter, we have in the present one analyzed the corresponding notions within psychology. It has been concluded that, to the psychologist, a stimulus is any event, within or upon a living object, which has a material effect upon that object only insofar as it produces conscious experience; and a response is any liberation of chemical energy by a living object, as produced by conscious experience.

The relationships among the biologist's 'stimulus' and 'response' and the 'stimulus' and 'response' of the psychologist have also been explored. It seems clear that the psychological response is a species of the biological; and it seems likely that the psychological stimulus is an instance of the biological stimulus—at any rate, it is generally so perceived.

To be emphasized here, as it was within the chapter proper, is the fact that conscious experience is being taken always as a purely physical event. There is thus no scientific impropriety in regarding it, upon occasion, as either a cause or an effect.

REFERENCES

Boring, E. G., H. S. Langfeld, and H. P. Weld. 1948. *Foundations of Psychology*. Wiley, New York; Chapman and Hall, London.

Bridgman, P. W. 1959. *The Way Things Are*. Harvard University Press, Cambridge, Massachusetts.

Brown, W., and H. C. Gilhousen. 1950. *College Psychology*. Prentice-Hall, New York.

Dunlap, K. 1928. *The Elements of Scientific Psychology*. Mosby, St. Louis.

English, H. B., and A. C. English. 1958. *A Comprehensive Dictionary of Psychological and Psychoanalytical Terms*. Longmans, Green; New York, London, and Toronto. Quotation by permission of David McKay Co., Inc.

Gibson, J. J. 1960. "The Concept of the Stimulus in Psychology." *Amer. Psychologist, 15*, 694–703.

Herman, D. T. 1957. "Perspectives in Psychology: II. What Is the Stimulus?" *Psychol. Rec., 7*, 70–72.

Hull, C. L. 1943. *Principles of Behavior*. Appleton-Century, New York and London.

James, W. 1896. *The Principles of Psychology*. Holt, New York.

Kantor, J. R. 1933. *A Survey of the Science of Psychology*. Principia Press, Bloomington, Indiana.

Keller, F. S., and W. N. Schoenfeld. 1950. *Principles of Psychology*. Appleton-Century-Crofts, New York and London.

Langfeld, H. S. 1931. "A Response Interpretation of Consciousness." *Psychol. Rev., 38*, 87–108.

Miller, N. E. 1959. In: Koch, S. (ed.) ; 1959; *Psychology: A Study of a Science* (Volume 2: *General Systematic Formulations, Learning, and Special Processes*) ; McGraw-Hill; New York, Toronto, and London.

Skinner, B. F. 1938. *The Behavior of Organisms.* Appleton-Century, New York and London.

Titchener, E. B. 1912. *An Outline of Psychology.* Macmillan, New York and London.

Tolman, E. C. 1932. *Purposive Behavior in Animals and Men.* Century, New York and London.

Watson, J. B. 1924. *Psychology from the Standpoint of a Behaviorist* (second edition). Lippincott, Philadelphia and London.

Watson, J. B. 1930. *Behaviorism* (revised edition). Norton, New York.

NOTES

The content of the foregoing chapter was summarized in the presidential address to the North Carolina Psychological Association in 1962, and outlined in some detail to the Dartmouth College Psychological Colloquium in the same year. An abstract of the former presentation can be found in *The Journal of the Elisha Mitchell Scientific Society,* 1962, *78,* 107. Since 1962, a relevant paper by W. M. O'Neil has appeared ("What Are Stimuli?", *Australian Journal of Psychology,* 1965, *17,* 109–116). It is interesting (and gratifying) that O'Neil's essential conclusion is this:

> Perhaps the only historical or logical restriction we need to impose is that "stimulus" [in the psychological sense] be applied only to that object, energy or other state of affairs which operates through the sense organs in its influence on behavior. [p. 114]

A brief note by M. Hocutt ("On the Alleged Circularity of Skinner's Concept of Stimulus," *Psychological Review,* 1967, *74,* 530–532) has criticized Gibson (1960, above); and there has been a brief reply (J. J. Gibson, "On the Proper Meaning of the Term 'Stimulus,'" *Psychological Review,* 1967, *74,* 533–534).

IV

THE CONCEPT OF 'LEARNING'

THE TWO foregoing chapters have discovered a somewhat unexpected distinction between the biological and
the psychological notions of 'stimulus' and 'response.'
The distinction is based upon the idea of 'conscious experience'; and that idea is one which has so far been established only in terms of a "pointing" definition.

It might seem advisable, in these circumstances, to
undertake immediately a formal analysis of the notion of
'conscious experience.' As it happens, however, such an
analysis is actually one which would be greatly facilitated by a prior examination of the concept of 'learning.' We shall accordingly turn just now to a consideration of the latter concept. Obviously, this consideration is
not only strategic in our approach to 'consciousness,'
but is of substantial interest in its own right, as well.

The present chapter, in scrutinizing and defining the
concept of 'learning,' will be divided into three main
sections. The first of these, essentially introductory in
nature, will scan critically the extant definitions of
'learning' and emphasize the need for a rigorous formulation. The second will suggest a tentative definition
of 'learning,' invoking historical evidence to validate
its suggestion. The third will address itself to the task of
refining that tentative definition and of producing finally
an acceptable formulation.

Preliminary Considerations

That the business of defining the concept of 'learning' is anything so formidable as a "task" is perhaps a rather startling thought. To anyone familiar with the psychological literature, however, this thought will not be surprising at all. It seems to be part of the lore of psychology that 'learning' never has been adequately defined and probably never will be. J. A. McGeoch, in the opening pages of his classical volume of 1942, provides an excellent illustration of the usual attitude:

> In a majority of cases there is agreement, without recourse to formal definition, upon whether or not a given change in behavior is an instance of learning. The formulation of a systematic definition is not easy, and the frequent attempts which have been made have not led to concordant results. There are, for one thing, a number of puzzling borderline cases which superficially look like learning, but which are not considered to be, such as maturation, work decrements, sensory adaptation, and drug effects. There is, likewise, the difficulty of framing a definition which will not be too heavily weighted with the framer's theoretical views to be acceptable to all. The important thing for the present purpose is that there is practically no doubt among the competent that the phenomena treated in this book are phenomena of learning. . . . What learning means, in more detail and aside from any formal definition, can best be seen from a presentation of the phenomena and of the conditions which determine them. [McGeoch 1942: 3–4]

Other instances of the same attitude are not difficult to find. We may turn logically enough, for example, to A. L. Irion's revision of the work just cited. Here we find not only a paraphrased version of the passage quoted above but also Irion's further assertion that:

. . . it is possible to define learning in either of two ways. On the one hand, we can define all changes of behavior which are *not* learned and define learning as the residual variability of behavior. On the other hand, we may take the more direct course and attempt to delimit precisely those behavioral changes which we desire to call learned. In practice, neither course has proved to be entirely satisfactory. [McGeoch and Irion 1952: 4]

McGeoch and Irion are joined by another psychologist who has been particularly concerned with the notion of 'learning,' E. R. Hilgard. Although Hilgard has subjected his own definition to careful revision over the past two or three decades (Hilgard and Marquis 1940: 347; Hilgard 1948: 4; Hilgard 1956: 3; Hilgard and Bower 1966: 2), his current formulation is one which is merely "offered provisionally" and which is "not formally satisfactory because of the many undefined terms in it" (Hilgard and Bower 1966: 2). Indeed, Hilgard has suggested elsewhere that:

A precise definition of learning is not necessary, so long as we agree that the inference to learning is made from changes in performance that are the result of training or experience, as distinguished from changes such as growth or fatigue and from changes attributable to the temporary state of the learner. The experiments themselves define the field ostensively. [Hilgard 1951: 518]

Rather more directly than the others, C. I. Hovland has stated the simple truth of the matter:

Although scores of definitions of learning have been proposed, none has become uniformly accepted. [Hovland 1951: 613]

And Hovland has been reinforced very recently by J. F. Hall (Hall 1966: 3–6).

The passages cited above not only substantiate the assertion that 'learning' is a difficult word to define properly. They also suggest some of the obstacles in the way of its correct definition. These obstacles have been mentioned only in a cursory fashion, however, and it is plainly a matter of considerable interest to identify them more exactly. The next few paragraphs, therefore, address themselves to the question, "Precisely what is wrong with the existing formulations of the concept of 'learning'?"

This question is obviously a broad one. In an effort to answer it, the literature in the area of learning has been surveyed rather thoroughly. Out of this survey has emerged the final conviction that there exist a half dozen rather standard inadequacies which, in one combination or another, act to cripple the extant definitions of 'learning.' In brief typification, these inadequacies can be described as (1) vagueness, (2) negative characterization, (3) dependence upon such terms as 'practice' or 'training,' (4) dependence upon such terms as 'improvement' or 'satisfaction,' (5) the arbitrary restriction of 'learning' to events satisfying theoretical stipulations, and (6) the arbitrary restriction of 'learning' to events in organisms possessing nervous systems. In more complete exposition, each of these deficiencies is— in its respective paragraph below—established as such and exemplified by citations from the literature.

Vagueness. It can hardly be denied that lack of clarity tends to invalidate a definition; and many a formulation of 'learning' suffers to a degree fatal to its purpose from an obscurity of one kind or another. In a passage obviously intended to be definitive, for example, Hull (1943: 68–69) sketches learning merely as a process which involves, somehow, the relative strengthening of certain "receptor-effector connections," by interaction with the environment. Lashley (1934) writes in a similar vein. Guthrie (1935: 2–3), too, is diffuse; and he lapses into the particular ambiguity of characterizing learning in terms of 'lasting' effects. In this lapse he is well accompanied, however. Bugelski (1956: 120) describes *"the formation of relatively permanent neural circuits,"* and Kimble (1961: 6) speaks of *"a relatively permanent change."* One wonders, "How lasting? How permanent?" Kellogg and Britt (1939), Spence (1951), and Deese (1952: 342) all provide additional examples of obscurity.

Negative Characterization. It is an accepted canon of logic that definition by exclusion is essentially worthless. All the same, this technique is employed by some who seek to define 'learning.' Irion has alluded to this fact in the passage cited above (McGeoch and Irion 1952: 4); and the earlier quotation from Hilgard (1951) has already provided something of an example. Other instances are not lacking (Hunter 1934; Guthrie 1935: 3; Hovland 1951; Hilgard 1956: 3; Hilgard and Bower 1966: 2).

Dependence Upon Such Terms as 'Practice' or 'Training.' Frequently, 'learning' is delineated in terms of 'practice,' 'training,' or something similar. Inasmuch as the customary meaning of any of these terms certainly depends upon 'learning' itself, very little is accomplished by such delineations. An insightful example is provided by Hilgard:

> The following definition may be offered provisionally: Learning is the process by which an activity originates or is changed through training procedures (whether in the laboratory or in the natural environment) as distinguished from changes by factors not attributable to training.
> The definition is unsatisfactorily evasive, and partly tautological, in leaving training procedures undefined. [Hilgard 1948: 4]

Other instances are numerous indeed (Guthrie 1935: 2–3; Hilgard and Marquis 1940: 347; McGeoch 1942:

3–4; Hilgard 1951; Brogden 1951; Hovland 1951; McGeoch and Irion 1952: 5; Kimble 1961: 6). An especially ambiguous variation upon this theme, it might be pointed out, is the definition which appeals to 'experience' (e.g., Guthrie 1935: 2; Hilgard 1951: 518): here, 'experience' is used as a synonym for 'training' or 'practice,' but the confusion is compounded by the inevitable suggestion of 'conscious experience.'

Dependence Upon Such Terms as 'Improvement' or 'Satisfaction.' To allege that learning, as a matter of definition, brings about improvement or produces satisfaction in the organism is now so recognized as unacceptable that extended discussion seems unnecessary. It is true, however, that such allegations can be found (Kellogg and Britt 1939; McGeoch 1942: 3–4; Brogden 1951).

The Arbitrary Restriction of 'Learning' to Events Satisfying Theoretical Stipulations. As McGeoch (1942: 3) has pointed out, behavioral theoreticians often have difficulty in excluding from their descriptive characterizations of 'learning' terms which are actually explanatory in nature. In a sense, we have already encountered this difficulty among those who hold that learning necessarily entails some sort of improvement or satisfaction. In a sense, too, we shall find it again among those who refer learning to specifically neural structures. More pointed examples come readily to hand, however. Thus, as long ago as 1903, Loeb defined his concept of 'associative memory' strictly in terms of the contiguity of stimuli and of what effect such contiguity was presumed to have in "our central nervous system" (Fearing 1930: 180). A half century later, Bugelski (1956: 120) proposed essentially the same definition. Formulations which do not commit themselves to a neurological theory but which do depend upon the notion of sheer contiguity are not uncommon. Skinner's "Law of Conditioning of Type S" is a case in point (Skinner 1938: 18). A related instance, but one which calls upon "reinforcement," is found in Kimble (1961: 6).

Arbitrary Restriction of 'Learning' to Events in Organisms Having Nervous Systems. As we have just seen, both Loeb and Bugelski introduce into their definitions of 'learning' not only stimulus contiguity but the nervous system as well. The tendency to assume a neural substrate for learning seems to be a common one (cf. also Cason 1937; Chappell 1940), but it goes without saying that learning cannot be denied, by definition, to rudimentary organisms. The question, "Can protozoa learn?", is a reasonable one.

At this juncture, then, the documentation required is completed. It appears that each of the alleged "common deficiencies" is indeed genuine. Without gainsaying the latter fact, it is, however, still important to recognize a point of logic: to have demonstrated that each of these deficiencies is common is not necessarily to have demonstrated that, collectively, they are exhaustive. Thus, although several inadequacies in the usual definitions of 'learning' have now been uncovered, there still remains the final question: "Is *every* extant formulation of 'learning' compromised by one or more of these inadequacies?"

To that question, the answer seems to be, "Yes." Such an answer has already been strongly suggested by the foregoing documentation itself. It is true, of course, that not every single existing definition of 'learning' has been specifically indicted by that documentation; but it is also true that virtually all of the major formulations, as well as a good many of the minor ones, have found themselves serving as examples of one kind of shortcoming or another. These formulations are both representative and influential, and it is improbable that even a comprehensive review would uncover a definition sufficiently unlike them to escape the criticisms to which they are vulnerable. Accordingly, no such review will be undertaken here. It will simply be presumed that there is in fact no adequate definition of 'learning' now in existence.

If this presumption is valid, the problem of bringing 'learning' into focus is indeed far from solution—so much so that the usual psychological attitude of pessimism on the issue seems almost to be justified.

A Definition of 'Learning'

One of the most dependable generalizations in all of psychology is this: When a problem which is known to be soluble continues to defy all efforts at solution, we can be almost certain that an unconscious assumption has been made as to the general direction in which the solution lies, and that that assumption is wrong. Surely, this generalization is a principle of relevance to us now.

For there can be no real doubt that 'learning' is definable. The concept exists, and it can be verbalized. At the same time, an impasse has obviously been reached in the attempt to realize it. The manifest implication of these facts is that those who have attempted to define 'learning' have fixated unknowingly upon a mistaken direction of endeavor. Our own task thus becomes one of shaking off the influence of this fixation and of finding a true course.

The procedure usually recommended in cases of this sort is an effective one. It is that of abandoning all direct efforts at solving the problem under consideration, of withdrawing psychologically from the area in which solution has already been attempted, and of seeking to visualize the entire problem anew. In terms of the instant question, it would obviously require that we resurvey the

whole realm of "learning," looking without bias for the
principle which unifies it.

Now, I wish to suggest that, when the realm of "learning" is contemplated in this open-minded fashion, the
fundamental notion behind the term itself becomes quite
clear. It is a notion not to be specified in terms of an
isolated sequence of overt, peripheral events in the life of
the organism. It is, furthermore, one not to be specified
in explicitly physiological or neurological terms. In actuality, the concept of 'learning'—like the psychological
concepts of 'stimulus' and 'response'—depends essentially upon the idea of 'conscious experience.' *Learning*,
one might say, *is the attachment of a new response to a
conscious experience, by conscious experience.*

There is no denying that this is a suggestion which,
seen against the backdrop of contemporary psychological
thought, has about it an element of the bizarre. Seen in
proper historical perspective, however, it becomes considerably more plausible. I now wish to limn some of that
perspective, hoping thus to endow the present suggestion
with a basic credibility. I shall consider three main
topics: (1) the classical notion of 'learning,' (2) the
meaning of 'learning' in Pavlovian systematics, and (3)
the modern usage of the word.

The Classical Concept of 'Learning.' The classical
meaning of 'learning,' and, in fact, its commonsense
meaning even today, is 'acquiring knowledge.' Thus,
when one "learns," he "stocks the mind" or "makes available to consciousness new facts and insights"; and he
does so by subjecting himself to a calculated flux of conscious experience.

This mode of thought was, of course, refined to the
point of systematic respectability by the British Empiri-
cists. In their hands, 'learning' became perforce 'the
development of new associations between ideas.' Thus,
the essential notion was that of one conscious event's

coming to evoke another by virtue of the fact that a basic contiguity between the two events had been enforced repeatedly by the environment itself. It is clear that the provisional definition of 'learning' which has been suggested above accommodates such a notion very nicely.

'Learning' in Pavlovian Systematics. Pavlov is generally pictured as a man who was completely scornful not only of British Empiricism but of any other kind of "mentalism," as well. Such a picture is actually somewhat overdrawn. In the first place, Pavlov was quite willing to recognize the existence of conscious experience, the "special *psychical* activity which we feel and apprehend in ourselves and which we suppose exists in animals by analogy with human beings" (Pavlov 1924: 173; see also Pavlov 1909: 218; 1932: 286; 1934: 245ff., 261). There is a little doubt, furthermore, that he considered this psychical activity to be efficacious in the behavior of the organism (Pavlov 1924: 177, 187; 1909: 207–208; 1934: 245–253). That Pavlov's objection to the terminology of consciousness and his dedication to the study of overt behavior represented not so much a metaphysical position as a methodological conviction is a fact verified repeatedly by Pavlov's own testimony:

> While making a detailed investigation of the digestive glands I had to busy myself also with the so-called psychical stimulation of the glands. When, together with one of my collaborators, I attempted a deeper analysis of this fact, at first in the generally accepted way, i.e., psychologically, visualizing the probable thoughts and feelings of the animal, I stumbled on a fact unusual in laboratory practice. I found myself unable to agree with my colleague; each of us stuck to his point of view, and we were unable to convince each other by certain experiments. This made me definitely reject any further psychological discussion of the subject, and I

decided to investigate it in a purely objective way,
externally. . . . [Pavlov 1924: 177]

. . . I [have] touched on the reasons that impelled us
to adopt a strictly objective method of investigating the
entire nervous activity in higher animals, i.e., of study-
ing it from the purely external factual aspect; this is in
keeping with the investigations in other branches of
natural science, and rules out fantastic speculation as
to the probable subjective state of the animals by analogy with ourselves. [Pavlov 1924: 188]

In fact, Pavlov's essential orientation is best suggested
by the questions he reports asking himself at the outset
of his experimental work:

Was it possible to discover an elementary *psychical*
phenomenon which at the same time could be fully and
rightly regarded as a purely *physiological* phenomenon? Was it possible to begin with it, and by a strictly
objective study (as generally done in physiology) of the
conditions of its emergence, its various complexities
and its disappearance, to obtain . . . an objective physiological picture of the entire higher nervous activity
in animals . . . ? [Pavlov 1934: 247; italics added]

As is well known, Pavlov answered these questions in the
affirmative; and the "conditioned reflex" became the elementary psychical phenomenon which was to be studied
with strict objectivity.

Pavlov himself seldom used the word 'learning.'
There is, however, little doubt that, to him, the conditioned reflex was the paradigm for learning in general
(e.g., Pavlov 1924: 197–198). The Pavlovian view of
learning is therefore simply the Pavlovian view of the
conditioned reflex, and we have already seen that the
latter was regarded fundamentally as a psychical entity.
It is worth mentioning now that Pavlov elaborated this

viewpoint in fairly specific terms. He made it clear, for example, that the conditioned stimulus was to be thought of as giving rise to sensation. Thus, he spoke repeatedly of the "signaling" function of such stimuli (1924: 187–189; 1932: 273); he pointed out that "In the animal, reality is signalized almost exclusively by stimulations . . . which come directly to the special cells of the visual, auditory or other receptors of the organism. This is what we, too, possess as impressions, sensations and notions of the world around us" (1934: 262); and, finally, he emphasized the function of the sensory "analyzers," remarking:

> These are what until now have been known as the sense organs. The physiological teaching of [i.e., concerning] these organs, as implied by their name, consists in large measure of subjective material, i.e., of observation and experimentation with the sensations and ideas of human beings, and is thus deprived of all the extraordinary means and advantages afforded by the objective study and the practically boundless field of experimentation on animals. [1909: 214]

Although Pavlov was somewhat less explicit about the sensory effects of the *unconditioned* stimulus, we end up with the impression that it, too, was presumed to evoke sensation. Thus, we find him stressing at one point the fact that reflexive salivation to buccal stimulation is mediated by a center in the medulla oblongata (1934: 248); and the legitimate inference would seem to be that conscious sensation is *not* entailed in this response. In other passages, however, there is emphasis upon the complexity of the unconditioned response and upon the presumption that it is elicited through mechanisms which are at least closely associated with the cerebral hemispheres (1932: 272–273). There is indeed the strong suggestion that the unconditioned stimulus, as well as the conditioned, must necessarily produce activity in the hemispheres themselves (1909: 208–212). It is significant, in this connection, that an authoritative contemporary source has recounted:

> According to the point of view adhered to in Pavlov's laboratories, the coupling of a temporary connection results from the blazing of a nervous pathway in the place where the irradiating excitations from the conditioned and unconditioned cortical centers meet. This meeting of the irradiating excitations is possible if both centers are activated simultaneously. Then the conditioned excitation can reach the cortical representation of the unconditioned center only when a focus of excitation arises in it which according to this point of view, plays a reinforcing role. [Voronin 1962: 189]

In point of fact, any obscurity in Pavlov's statements about the unconditioned stimulus, as well as any other obscurity at all in his characterization of the conditioned reflex as a "psychical phenomenon," can be dissipated by turning to a final source of data: Pavlov's assertions concerning the relationship of the conditioned reflex to the phenomenon of "learning by association" as traditionally envisaged. Two examples will make his position in this matter clear:

> . . . *the conditioned reflex* . . . is a temporary nervous connection between numberless agents in the animal's external environment, which are received by the receptors of the given animal, and the definite activities of the organism. This phenomenon is called by psychologists *association*. [Pavlov 1932: 272]

> Thus, the temporary nervous connection is the most universal physiological phenomenon both in the animal world and in ourselves. At the same time it is a psychological phenomenon—that which the psychologist calls association, whether it be combinations derived from all manner of actions or impressions, or combinations

derived from letters, words and thoughts. Are there any grounds for differentiation, for distinguishing between that which the physiologist calls the temporary connection and that which the psychologist terms association? They are fully identical; they merge and absorb each other. Psychologist themselves seem to recognize this, since they (at least, some of them) have stated that the experiments with conditioned reflexes provide a solid foundation for associative psychology, i.e., psychology which regards association as the base of psychical activity. This is . . . true. . . . [Pavlov 1934: 251]

Pavlov could hardly have been more explicit: the conditioned reflex *was* "learning by association." Our impression that both the conditioned and the unconditioned stimuli were to be thought of as producing sensation is thus verified. More importantly, the conclusion that 'learning,' even to Pavlov, consisted of 'the attachment of a new response *to* a conscious experience, *by* conscious experience,' appears to be virtually forced upon us. It is true that, in Pavlov's thinking, the new response was a simple, overt act, rather than the complex subjective response of traditional associationism. It was upon this fact that his method was built, however, and by it that his pride was sustained.

The Modern Concept of 'Learning.' It can be said not unfairly that the modern concept of 'learning' is the behavioristic concept: the modern definitions, behavioristic definitions. It can also be said that modern, behavioristic definitions comprise essentially the entire realm of the existing definitions of 'learning.' For it appears that the prebehavioristic psychologist, for his part, felt very little need for any formal declaration of meaning. 'Learning' meant what 'learning' had always meant. The need for explication seems to have arisen only later,

as a part of the general behavioristic urge toward rein-
terpretation.

Under these circumstances, it is quite possible for us
now to obtain a cross-section of *modern* definitions, simply by looking back at our own earlier review of *existing*
definitions. It is true that, looking back in this fashion,
we rediscover a somewhat cryptic collection of items. Not
only is it one which is classified merely on the basis of
nature of definitional error; it is also one which runs
more to oblique reference than to full citation. In spite of
these shortcomings, however, it is a collection which
serves adequately to delineate the basic pattern of the
contemporary conception of learning. That pattern implies, of course, that, whatever learning may amount to
in precise detail, it consists essentially in the connection
of a new response to a given stimulus—with the process
of connection depending somehow upon events which are
themselves stimuli.

I say, "of course"; for, although it might be possible to
argue against this rendition of the present-day concept
of 'learning,' the scope of legitimate argument would
seem to be limited. Modern psychology is a stimulus-response psychology; and this is the sort of stimulus-response formulation to which it is virtually forced. The
given statement represents, I think, the area of mutual
agreement among the many rather similar statements
offered in recent years. Upon this basis we may therefore
proceed.

Now, if the psychologist meant what he thinks he
means by 'stimulus' and 'response,' his fundamental
definition of 'learning' would plainly constitute a revo-
lutionary break with the past. The psychologist believes
he is using 'stimulus' and 'response' as the biologist
uses them, without any reference at all to 'consciousness'; and, if he were correct in that belief, he would

obviously be defining 'learning' itself without appeal to 'conscious experience.' In sharp contrast, the traditional notion of 'learning' depends precisely, as we have seen, upon the idea of 'consciousness.' The discrepancy between the two conceptualizations is thus patent, as is the ostensible novelty of the modern definition.

Actually, of course, the modern definition is not new. As Chapter III has demonstrated, the psychologist's notions of 'stimulus' and 'response' are in fact basically different from those of the biologist. Unlike the biologist, the psychologist has the very idea of 'conscious experience' firmly embedded within his meanings for both 'stimulus' and 'response.' The effect of this circumstance is to reduce the modern, behavioristic definition of 'learning' to orthodoxy, and thus to the formulation suggested here. *Once again, 'learning' becomes 'the attachment of a new response to a conscious experience, by conscious experience.'*

Now, strictly speaking, this logic disposes, once and for all, of the modern concept of 'learning.' It establishes the fact that the latter notion, like the Pavlovian notion, is precisely the classical notion; and it thus secures the point that the definition of 'learning' advanced earlier is consonant with history as a whole. Valid though it may be, however, such naked logic seems rather ineffectual against the habits of thought of half a century. One finds himself casting about for elaboration and support, for substantive verification of the abstract conclusion. What we appear to need is two or three good instances, cases showing plainly that *even the modern psychologist rejects the possibility of learning in a system presumed to lack the capacity for conscious experience.*

As it happens, at least two such examples stand out rather clearly from the scientific literature. Each seems to be worth developing at some length, and each will be so

developed in the remainder of this section. The first is
concerned with the question of whether or not learning
ever occurs in one-celled organisms; the second, with the
issue of "spinal conditioning." Together, these examples
tend, I think, to verify the conclusion to which our logic
has already led us.

Learning in One-Celled Organisms. Earlier in the
present chapter, it was asserted that the question of
whether or not protozoa can learn is a reasonable one.
Psychology in general has seemed to agree with this assertion, for the problem of learning in single-celled animals is given serious attention in both the journals and
the textbooks. In spite of this ostensible open-mindedness,
however, there seems to exist among psychologists an
underlying resistance to the notion that such learning
ever actually occurs. Thus, as appropriate documentation will presently show, patterns of behavior which
would be taken without hesitation to represent the occurrence of learning in human beings, in rats, or even in
cockroaches (cf. Warden, Jenkins, and Warner 1940:
796–800; Minami and Dallenbach 1946) are generally
discounted and dismissed when they manifest themselves
in protozoa. No reason is ever advanced for this curious
discrimination. It is difficult to believe, however, that it
reflects merely a skepticism concerning the structural
qualifications of the protozoon for a kind of modification
in activity which does *not* depend on conscious experience; for it is quite possible that the structure of a single
cell provides all of the elements necessary for such a
process. Almost certainly, the explanation lies instead in
the direction already suggested: psychologists find it
next to impossible to concede consciousness to unicellular
organisms, and thus they cannot accept the idea of learning (with its tacitly presumed dependence upon consciousness) in such organisms.

The assertion that psychologists generally resist the

ascription of learning to single-celled animals is one
which is not difficult to support. Documentation might
well begin with the pioneer study reported by Mast and
Pusch in 1924. As is rather well known, these investiga-
tors found that an amoeba becomes increasingly efficient,
with successive exposures to the situation, in moving
away from a patch of strong illumination. The organism's activities are precisely those which would be described as "escape learning" in a higher animal. All the
same, both Mast himself and those who have reviewed his
work have actively opposed the inference that learning
does in fact occur (Maier and Schneirla 1935: 21, 33–35;
Warden, Jenkins, and Warner 1940: 173–179).

A second example is embodied in another well-known
report: Jennings's description of the behavior of stentor
(Jennings 1906: 170–179). It will be recalled that this
protozoon, in the face of prolonged exposure to grains of
carmine or India ink, goes through a succession of responses of a more and more vigorous nature: "The organism 'tries' one method of action; if this fails, it tries
another, till one succeeds" (Jennings 1906: 177). Left
unstimulated for a while, furthermore, stentor responds to new stimulation, not by repeating the whole
sequence of behavior, but by making one of the later
responses in the series (Jennings 1906: 175). Finally,
stentor shows a striking sort of negative adaptation
which "is not due to fatigue, either of the contractile
apparatus or of the perceptive power" (Jennings 1906:
173). "Is the change in the behavior of Stentor in accord-
ance with its past history a phenomenon in any wise
similar in character to the learning of a higher organism?" asks Jennings. "In judging of this question we
must rely, of course, entirely upon objective evidence;—
upon what can be actually observed. When this is done, it
is hard to discover any ground for making a distinction
in principle between the two cases" (Jennings 1906:

178). In spite of this behavioral identity, however, Jennings ultimately refrains from attributing learning to protozoa. He enunciates his famous "law of the resolution of physiological states" and expresses his conviction that the law is a principle valid for lower as well as higher organisms; but the "phenomena which we commonly call memory, association, habit formation, and learning," which display the "operations of this law . . . on a vast scale," are mentioned only in connection with the higher organisms (Jennings 1906: 291).

A final example of the common reluctance to ascribe learning to unicellular organisms can be found in the history of research on the behavior of paramecia. Prominent in that history are the early experiments of S. Smith and of Day and Bentley, which suggested that paramecia might be capable of learning a bending-reaction (Maier and Schneirla 1935: 33–34; Warden, Jenkins, and Warner 1940: 175–176). These studies were criticized by Buytendijk, who argued that the experimental animals might simply have undergone an increase in physical flexibility, an increase which, he showed, could be produced artificially (Maier and Schneirla 1935: 34; Warden, Jenkins, and Warner 1940: 177). Inasmuch as Day and Bentley had in fact provided long rest periods for their subjects (as a precaution against just this sort of artifact), we might reasonably expect Buytendijk's criticism to have been largely ignored. Quite to the contrary. To Maier and Schneirla, for example, the findings of Day and Bentley merely indicate that "Such a protoplasmic change [as the one suggested by Buytendijk] evidently survives for some time" (1935: 34; cf. also Warden, Jenkins, and Warner 1940: 175–177). Again, somewhat later, French (1940) demonstrated what was to all appearances "trial and error learning" in paramecia. His demonstration, however, along with others less impressive, has simply been regarded with a kind of diffuse skepticism (see Katz and Deterline 1958). Indeed, such skepticism has been the usual attitude toward any report of learning in unicellular organisms (Maier and Schneirla 1935: 34–35; Warden, Jenkins, and Warner 1940: 176–179; Jensen 1957; Katz and Deterline 1958).

The widespread existence of this unwillingness to regard as evidence of learning in some organisms the same manifestations which are readily accepted as proof of learning in others, provides (I believe) considerable support for the proposition that the concept of 'learning' incorporates that of 'conscious experience.' That support is not all that is available, however. Additional, rather impressive evidence can be found in the second area mentioned earlier: that of "spinal conditioning." It is thus appropriate that we turn our attention now to this other line of evidence.

"Spinal Conditioning." Until the 1930s, it had been a continuous and universal presumption, having a number of bases in empirical observation and common sense, that the spinal cord is incapable of mediating learned responses. During the 1930s, nevertheless, P. S. Shurrager and E. A. Culler undertook to put the matter to experimental test. They worked with spinal dogs; and presently they reported that, in surprising fact, conditioning was indeed possible with such preparations (Shurrager and Culler 1940). During the following two decades, Shurrager published repeatedly in this area, with various collaborators, and cited generally positive findings (see Dykman and Shurrager 1956 for a helpful bibliography). Although he has freely admitted that many animals fail to show spinal conditioning, Shurrager has, nevertheless, contended that many others do and that the phenomenon is thus a real one (e.g., see Shurrager and Shurrager 1950).

The principal critic of Shurrager's position has been W. N. Kellogg. Along with his associates, Kellogg has undertaken a number of control experiments and, in the light of their results, expressed considerable skepticism about spinal conditioning (cf. especially Kellogg 1947; Deese and Kellogg 1949). Kellogg's group has, however, been almost alone in its active opposition (although see Pinto and Bromiley 1950) ; and, in the main, the group's findings have not been particularly impressive. At least on paper, therefore, the evidence against spinal conditioning is far from overwhelming (see Morgan and Stellar 1950: 440–446; Morgan 1951; Osgood 1953: 479–481).

Now, considering the fact that "The implications of the [positive] findings on spinal conditioning for physiology, neuropsychology, and the psychology of learning are so far-reaching that they strike at the very roots of the general conception of the nervous system" (Kellogg, Deese, Pronko, and Feinberg 1947), these findings have had remarkably little impact upon the scientific literature. When they were first published, for example, there was none of the immediate and widespread attempt at replication which usually follows the report of a significant new phenomenon. Even the negative evidence offered by Kellogg and his associates was slow in coming forward. When it did arrive, moreover, it evoked no greater interest than had the positive. In short, no one took spinal conditioning very seriously.

All of this constitutes a curious state of affairs. It is one that can be explained rather readily, however, in terms of the hypothesis that the notion of 'learning' pivots upon that of 'consciousness.' "Everyone knows" that the spinal cord is purely unconscious in function. Thus—granting the tacit premise that any form of learning depends upon consciousness—"everyone knew" that spinal conditioning was impossible, anyway. Negative data of a formal sort were not even required. The cause of spinal conditioning was lost from the start.

Of our two scientific case histories, it might be noted, it is the present one which is the more compelling. The adamant might possibly maintain that learning in protozoa is out of the question simply because of the structural limitations of these organisms, even though this contention is in fact implausible. The instance of spinal conditioning, however, avoids even this unlikely alternative explanation. The spinal cord provides plenty of neural complexity. Thus, we can evidently have only one reason for rejecting the idea of learning as mediated by spinal centers. It is our own intuitive conviction that, however elaborate these centers and their connections may be, there is no consciousness in them.

Having now adduced concrete evidence in support of its basic logic, the present subsection, on the modern concept of 'learning,' comes to a close. To paraphrase a summary statement made earlier, it is evident that the modern notion of 'learning' is identical with the Pavlovian notion, and that both are neither more nor less than what the notion of "learning" has always been thought to be. The words in which the essential idea may be stated are these: *'Learning' is 'the attachment of a new response to a conscious experience, by conscious experience.'*

The Definition of 'Learning'

The formulation with which the previous section comes to a close is one which appears repeatedly and unchangingly throughout the section itself. Such repetition perhaps endows it with an aura of finality which it does not truly deserve. It will be recalled that, from the start, this particular definition has been labeled as "tentative."

It is the object of the present section to bring this definition of 'learning' to some degree of actual finality, In pursuit of that object, I now wish to make just two comments, and to revise the formulation as seems necessary in the light of each. The first point is a comparatively minor one, having to do with the initial few words of the definition. The second, which refers to the final three words, is somewhat more substantial.

'The Attachment of a New Response. . . .' The initial portion of the definition specifies that 'learning' is 'the attachment of a new response to a conscious experience'; and this is a pronouncement having a certain ring of orthodoxy about it. Only its last two words tend to jar: one expects 'stimulus' instead of 'conscious experience' —but this is a disparity which has now been rationalized extensively. A word that is *not* surprising in this context is 'response,' for the idea of 'response' is central in every contemporary definition of 'learning.' All the same, it is precisely the word 'response' about which we ought to have at least some misgivings.

'Response' has now, by office of the two preceding chapters, acquired not only one but two fairly precise meanings. As it happens, either of these meanings may be read into the term in its present context. The phrase, 'the attachment of a new response to a conscious experience,' already stipulates that the response is one to be evoked by consciousness, in any case. In terms of either of these two meanings, however, a response must represent the liberation of chemical energy; and it is this fact that makes the word 'response' a problem here. We are hardly certain yet that every single activity which can be connected to a conscious experience by a process called "learning" does consist, literally, in the liberation of such energy. Thus, for example, most if not all of our cognitive activities are "learned": but is the occurrence of a thought, say, actually an instance of the release of chemical energy? Conceivably, it is not. It would generally be presumed to be, however; and, in all likelihood, it is. The same sort of opinion, furthermore, would attach itself to the other varieties of cognitive function. To use the word 'response' in a definition of 'learning' consequently seems quite defensible, and no change is indicated for the present. All the same, it is worth noting here that there may some day be reason to replace 'response' with 'activity' or 'effect.'

'. . . *By Conscious Experience.*'   The second comment concerns the phrase, 'by conscious experience.' More especially, it has to do with the single word 'by,' a word having a great multiplicity of meanings. The general intention of the word right here is clearly that of 'through the agency of.' Even granting that fact, however, the phrase, 'by conscious experience,' remains equivocal. There are several ways in which a new response can become attached to a conscious experience through the agency of conscious experience, and they are not all instances of learning. We therefore have the task of specifying just which ones are.

In approaching this task, it is useful to visualize for a moment the sequence of events constituting the ordinary case of learning. That sequence is basically simple. It begins with the circumstance that a given conscious event elicits a given response (which may actually, as a special case, be no response at all). It then proceeds through a phase in which this event and its contingent response are accompanied on a number of occasions by a second and differing conscious experience. When, at the close of that phase, the first sort of conscious event is again made to occur alone, it is found to have a new response, rather than its original one, attached to it. That is the end of the sequence: learning has taken place.

So much is pure description. From this description there can nevertheless be drawn a number of thoroughly noncontroversial conclusions. In the first place, it is indisputable that a change has occurred in the pathway of response beyond the locus of the first conscious experience. Secondly, it is just as undeniable that this change has been wrought by the effects of the second sort of conscious event. Finally, a certain spatial relationship within the responding organism is necessarily implied. The second conscious experience, being an event different from the first one, must have expressed its effects over a pathway somewhat different from that activated by the first one. In fact, its effects must have impinged upon the first response circuit from without and managed to alter the first circuit only by virtue of this impact. It would appear, then, that the process to which the word 'learning' refers is essentially the attachment of a new response to a conscious experience, *owing to the impingement of the effects of a second conscious experience upon the pathway of response to the first experience.*

It will be noted that this latter statement has arisen from the consideration of a highly generalized instance of learning. The statement, therefore, possesses a substantial generality of its own. For example, it retains its validity in the face of any temporal relationship whatsoever between the two conscious events concerned. Somewhat more uniquely, it also avoids any dependence upon "the nervous system," or upon such terms as 'training,' 'practice,' 'improvement,' or 'satisfaction.' It is free, I think, of any theoretical suppositions. All in all, it would appear to afford a pleasantly prompt reply to our question as to the sense of the word 'by' in the original, tentative definition of 'learning.'

Unfortunately, though, matters are really not quite so settled. For all its generality, the "ordinary case of learning" upon which our logic has been based is limited in one important respect. It does indeed represent the usual sort of learning situation: the kind in which two separate conscious experiences are involved. It does *not*, however, represent the remaining sort of situation: the kind in which the "second" experience is simply a continuation of the first. Such cases are actually rather common. Indeed, they are well typified by the usual instance of "escape learning," in which an animal is subjected without warning, on successive trials, to a noxious stimulus; must suffer that simulus, on each trial, until the "correct" response is forthcoming; and, characteristically, escapes the noxious stimulus more and more quickly, as the trials progress. Here is an acknowledged form of "learning," yet one which seems to elude our incumbent definition. The first conscious experience is easy enough to identify: it is the effect of the noxious stimulus. But where is the second, separate, impinging experience?

Patently, there is none. Clearly, then, the definition needs to be enlarged; and a number of expansions come to mind. I should like to suggest, however, that the most plausible of these would assign to the single conscious experience in this case, both the "cue" function of the usual first experience and the "impingement" function of the usual second one. I would thus argue that, when we talk about "learning" in the special situation now under consideration, we assume that the sensation produced by the noxious stimulus is having two separable effects. In the first place, it is serving (especially during its early moments) as a signal or cue, and thus producing impulses in a specific efferent pathway. In the second place, it is tending (especially as it persists) to evoke diffuse, nonspecific impulses, which bombard essentially all efferent pathways—including the particular one just mentioned.

The plausibility of this argument resides in its agreement with intuition. In a commonsense way, our picture of what is going on within an animal as it learns to escape from a noxious stimulus is this: At the onset of the stimulus, the animal begins to respond in a particular fashion; as the animal continues to respond in this fashion, however, it continues to be punished by the noxious stimulus —until this initial pattern of response is disrupted, and a new pattern supervenes; the new pattern, in its turn, continues to sustain the punishing effects of the same stimulus—and a third pattern replaces it; and so on— until the noxious stimulus ceases. The change in sensation contingent upon the cessation of the noxious stimulus is perhaps a genuine "second" experience, and the animal's acquisition of the correct response is perhaps an instance of learning as we already have it defined. Before making the *correct* response, however, the animal seems to have learned *not* to make several other sorts of response. And, intuitively, we see it as having done so because the persisting pain of the noxious stimulus acted to discourage the response initiated by the pain itself. In short, we do indeed conceive of the single conscious experience involved as providing both a "cue" effect and an "impingement" effect. If we did not, we would not think of 'learning.' We would think instead of 'adaptation,' or 'fatigue,' or 'accumulation of inhibition.'

If the foregoing argument is persuasive, the definitional change it implies is a minor one. The concept of 'learning' remains fundamentally the same, whether in the usual case or in the special case just considered; and a final statement of that concept, couched in a manner to cover both contingencies, is this: *'Learning' is 'an alteration in the nature of the response attached to a given conscious experience, due to the impingement of effects from a second conscious experience, or from the same one, upon some portion of the pathway of response to the first experience.'*

Summary and Conclusion

The present chapter has taken note of the lack of an acceptable definition for 'learning.' Pointing out that, in both historical and contemporary thinking, the characteristic feature of 'learning' is its dependence upon the conjunction of conscious experiences, this chapter has offered a tentative definition: 'Learning' is 'the attachment of a new response *to* a conscious experience, *by* conscious experience.' The tentative definition has been made more precise, without (it is believed) loss of adequate generality. The formulation finally offered is this: 'Learning' is 'an alteration in the nature of the response attached to a given conscious experience, due to the impingement of effects from a second conscious experience, or from the same one, upon some portion of the pathway of response to the first experience.'

It may be recalled that, at the beginning of the present chapter, it was asserted that an analysis of the idea of 'conscious experience' would be greatly facilitated by a prior analysis of the idea of 'learning.' The sense in which this assertion is true has now become evident; and that sense is a somewhat perverse one. It now appears that, when we come to define 'conscious experience,' we cannot utilize in our definition the term 'learning'; for 'learning' itself depends on 'conscious experience.' Inasmuch as we should almost certainly have been inclined toward the error thus anticipated, our analysis of 'learning' has perhaps been useful.

REFERENCES

Brogden, W. J. 1951. "Animal Studies of Learning." In: Stevens, S. S. (ed.) ; 1951; *Handbook of Experimen-*

tal Psychology; Wiley, New York; and Chapman and Hall, London.

Bugelski, B. R. 1956. *The Psychology of Learning*. Holt, New York.

Cason, H. 1937. "The Concepts of Learning and Memory." *Psychol. Rev., 44*, 54–61.

Chappell, M. N. 1940. "The Inadequacy of the Kellogg-Britt Definition of Learning." *Psychol. Rev., 47*, 90–94.

Deese, J. 1952. *The Psychology of Learning*. McGraw-Hill; New York, London, and Toronto.

Deese, J., and W. N. Kellogg. 1949. "Some New Data on the Nature of 'Spinal Conditioning.' " *J. Comp. and Physiol. Psychol., 42*, 157–160.

Dykman, R. A., and P. S. Shurrager. 1956. "Successive and Maintained Conditioning in Spinal Carnivores." *J. Comp. and Physiol. Psychol., 49*, 27–35.

Fearing, F. 1930. *Reflex Action*. Williams and Wilkins, Baltimore.

French, J. W. 1940. "Trial and Error Learning in Paramecium." *J. Exper. Psychol., 26*, 609–613.

Guthrie, E. R. 1935. *The Psychology of Learning*. Harper, New York and London.

Hall, J. F. 1966. *The Psychology of Learning*. Lippincott, Philadelphia.

Hilgard, E. R. 1948. *Theories of Learning*. Appleton-Century-Crofts, New York and London.

Hilgard, E. R. 1951. "Methods and Procedures in the Study of Learning." In: Stevens, S. S. (ed.) ; 1951; *Handbook of Experimental Psychology*; Wiley, New York; and Chapman and Hall, London.

Hilgard, E. R. 1956. *Theories of Learning* (second edition). Appleton-Century-Crofts, New York.

Hilgard, E. R., and G. H. Bower. 1966. *Theories of Learning* (third edition). Appleton-Century-Crofts, New York.

Hilgard, E. R., and D. G. Marquis. 1940. *Conditioning and Learning*. Appleton-Century, New York and London.

Hovland, C. I. 1951. "Human Learning and Retention." In: Stevens, S. S. (ed.) ; 1951; *Handbook of Experimental Psychology*; Wiley, New York; and Chapman and Hall, London.

Hull, C. L. 1943. *Principles of Behavior*. Appleton-Century, New York and London.

Hunter, W. S. 1934. "Learning: IV. Experimental Studies of Learning." In: Murchison, C. (ed.); 1934; *Handbook of General Experimental Psychology*; Clark University Press, Worcester, Massachusetts; and Oxford University Press, London.

Jennings, H. S. 1906. *Behavior of the Lower Organisms*. Columbia University Press, New York (Macmillan, agents).

Jensen, D. D. 1957. "Experiments on 'Learning' in Paramecia." *Science, 125,* 191–192.

Katz, M. S., and W. A. Deterline. 1958. "Apparent Learning in the Paramecium." *J. Comp. and Physiol. Psychol., 51,* 243–247.

Kellogg, W. N. 1947. "Is 'Spinal Conditioning' Conditioning? Reply to 'A Comment.' " *J. Exper. Psychol., 37,* 263–265.

Kellogg, W. N., and S. H. Britt. 1939. "Structure or Function in the Definition of Learning?" *Psychol. Rev., 46,* 186–198.

Kellogg, W. N., J. Deese, N. H. Pronko, and M. Feinberg. 1947. "An Attempt to Condition the *Chronic* Spinal Dog." *J. Exper. Psychol., 37,* 99–117.

Kimble, G. A. 1961. *Hilgard and Marquis' Conditioning and Learning*. Appleton-Century-Crofts, New York.

Lashley, K. S. 1934. "Learning: II. Nervous Mechanisms in Learning." In: Murchison, C. (ed.); 1934; *Handbook of General Experimental Psychology*; Clark University Press, Worcester, Massachusetts; and Oxford University Press, London.

Maier, N. R. F., and T. C. Schneirla. 1935. *Principles of Animal Psychology*. McGraw-Hill, New York and London.

McGeoch, J. A. 1942. *The Psychology of Human Learning* & McGeoch, J. A., and A. L. Irion. 1952. *The Psychology of Human Learning* (second edition). Longmans, Green; New York, London, and Toronto. (Quotations by permission of David McKay Co., Inc.

Minami, H., and K. M. Dallenbach. 1946. "The Effect of Activity upon Learning and Retention in the Cockroach, *Periplaneta americana.*" *Amer. J. Psychol., 59,* 1–58.

Morgan, C. T. 1951. "The Psychophysiology of Learning." In: Stevens, S. S. (ed.) ; 1951; *Handbook of Experimental Psychology*; Wiley, New York; and Chapman and Hall, London.

Morgan, C. T., and E. Stellar. 1950. *Physiological Psychology.* McGraw-Hill; New York, Toronto, and London.

Osgood, C. E. 1953. *Method and Theory in Experimental Psychology.* Oxford University Press, New York.

Pavlov, I. P. 1909. "Natural Science and the Brain." In: Pavlov, I. P.; 1957; *Experimental Psychology and Other Essays*; Philosophical Library, New York.

Pavlov, I. P. 1924. "Lectures on the Work of the Cerebral Hemispheres." In: Pavlov, I. P.; 1957; *Experimental Psychology and Other Essays;* Philosophical Library, New York.

Pavlov, I. P. 1932. "Physiology of the Higher Nervous Activity." In: Pavlov, I. P.; 1957; *Experimental Psychology and Other Essays;* Philosophical Library, New York.

Pavlov, I. P. 1934. "The Conditioned Reflex." In: Pavlov, I. P.; 1957; *Experimental Psychology and Other Essays;* Philosophical Library, New York.

Pinto, T., and R. B. Bromiley. 1950. "A Search for 'Spinal Conditioning' and for Evidence That It Can Become a Reflex." *J. Exper. Psychol., 40,* 121–130.

Shurrager, P. S., and E. A. Culler. 1940. "Conditioning in the Spinal Dog." *J. Exper. Psychol., 26,* 133–159.

Shurrager, P. S., and H. C. Shurrager. 1950. "Comment on 'A Search for "Spinal Conditioning" and for Evidence That It Can Become a Reflex.' " *J. Exper. Psychol., 40,* 135–137.

Skinner, B. F. 1938. *The Behavior of Organisms.* Appleton-Century, New York and London.

Spence, K. W. 1951. "Theoretical Interpretations of Learning." In: Stevens, S. S. (ed.) ; 1951; *Handbook of Ex-*

perimental Psychology; Wiley, New York; and Chapman and Hall, London.

Voronin, L. G. 1962. "Some Results of Comparative-Physiological Investigations of Higher Nervous Activity." *Psychol. Bull., 59,* 161–195.

Warden, C. J., T. N. Jenkins, and L. H. Warner. 1940. *Comparative Psychology,* Volume II: *Plants and Invertebrates.* Ronald Press, New York.

NOTES

The greater part of this paper was presented to the Psychology Colloquium of the North Carolina State University in 1963. Since then, a relevant paper by A. A. Buerger and A. M. Dawson has appeared ("Spinal Kittens: Long-Term Increases in Electromyograms Due to a Conditioning Routine," *Physiology and Behavior,* 1968, *3,* 99–103). In discussing positive findings, Buerger and Dawson express an attitude consonant with the conclusions of the present paper: "On the basis of the above data, a decision that spinal animals are able to be conditioned or able to learn depends largely on one's definitions of conditioning and learning" (pp. 102–103).

V

'CONSCIOUS EXPERIENCE'

IN THE light of the preceding chapters, it appears that the notion of 'conscious experience' is not only a concept of great intrinsic interest, but one of basic systematic importance as well. It has so far been convenient to allow that notion to remain on a logical level which is entirely primitive. Plainly, however, it ought to be examined closely.

The present essay undertakes the requisite examination. The essay begins by alluding briefly to previous attempts to define 'consciousness,' pointing out that those attempts have been unsuccessful. It then follows historically the evolution of a "criterion of consciousness" which has, in the absence of a true definition of 'conscious experience,' come to be rather generally accepted. It goes on to show, however, that this criterion is in fact illusory. Finally, it turns to what is thus the persisting question of the meaning of 'conscious experience,' and seeks to give that question rigorous and acceptable reply.

Previous Attempts To Define 'Consciousness'

Until about the beginning of the twentieth century, the effort to define 'conscious experience' was largely a philosophical enterprise. It must be said that, during this phase, the effort did not go well. It produced a literature which is virtually meaningless today and which was probably equally obscure to its own authors. The philosophers of the twentieth century itself have, furthermore, continued to handle the problem of 'consciousness' in much the same manner. All in all, there seems to be an element of justice in K. S. Lashley's summary dismissal of the philosophical approach: "Metaphysicians and theologians have spent so many years weaving fairy tales about . . . [consciousness] . . . that they have come to believe one another's phantasies" (Lashley 1958: 2).

It was during the early years of the twentieth century, of course, that the discipline of psychology was making an especially vigorous attempt to divorce itself entirely from that of philosophy. In spite of the vigor of the effort, the separation was at first incomplete; and the psychological scene was dominated for some time by the "philosopher-psychologists." These men essayed their own delineations of 'consciousness,' but they found it virtually impossible to free themselves from the philosophical tradition of nonsense. R. B. Perry, for example, approached and (he felt) finally reached a "definition of consciousness" in the following fashion:

> . . . the field of psychology comes into view only when an incomplete experience is recognized as such from the standpoint of an experience regarded as objective. The corrected or discredited experience so determined critically in an experience of things, is regarded as merely my experience, and may be analyzed as such. But we must have passed beyond the psychical to become aware of it. These psychical data cannot be called things or reals in the same sense as the standard objects, for they are completed and replaced by the latter. *We therefore provide a radically different category for them, and recognize that their content is common to themselves and to things, while their specific character*

is given them by their limitations and context. [Perry 1904: 289; italics added]

Another instance comes from E. B. Holt, who devoted an entire volume to *The Concept of Consciousness*. Holt came to the principal conclusion that:

> In fine, the consciousness that depends on any given living organism is the sum total of all neutral entities to which that living organism responds, and it is the system of these entities in just such and such quantity and just such spatial and temporal arrangement as the environment and the responses themselves define. [Holt 1914: 183–184]

That conclusion was elaborated and clarified in the following terms:

> Indeed it should be obvious that the *definition* of consciousness is its only possible criterion. If consciousness is that cross-section of the realm of *being* to which the organism specifically responds, then the criterion of consciousness is the specific response; and the animal or the plant, like the human being, is conscious of that to which it specifically responds. [Holt 1914: 205–206]

Here, had 'specific response' been given secure meaning, the formulation might possibly have tended toward significance; but no such meaning was in fact forthcoming.

As the twentieth century wore on, psychology proper assumed the burden of 'conscious experience.' It was a burden which became, as psychology began to embrace behaviorism, increasingly discomfiting. All the same, it was not entirely abandoned. E. C. Tolman, for one, ventured a behavioristic definition of 'consciousness.' His version, tending to follow the lead already established by Holt, went as follows:

> . . . *wherever an organism at a given moment of stimulation shifts then and there from being ready to re-*

spond in some relatively less differentiated way to being
ready to respond in some relatively more differentiated
way, there is consciousness. [Tolman 1927: 435]

This formulation, like Holt's own, patently suffered from
extreme nebulosity. The same sort of diffuseness characterized the definition offered by K. S. Lashley (even
though Lashley, as we have seen, was later to become
caustic over the "phantasies" of others). His contention
was:

Consciousness consists of particular patterns and se-
quences of the reactions [of an organism] interacting
among themselves and the attributes of consciousness
are definable in terms of the relations and succession of
the reactions. [Lashley 1923: 341] . . . [Complex]
reactions are awareness. [Lashley 1923: 336]

In fairness, it should be said that vagueness of this sort
did not always characterize behavioristic proposals.
W. S. Hunter, for one, offered a definition which was entirely succinct:

The irreversible relationship SP [sensory process]-*LR*
[language response] *is the phenomenon termed "con-*
sciousness." [Hunter 1924: 11]

It should be acknowledged at once that Hunter gave a
somewhat generalized meaning to the term 'language
response.' All the same, it remains a fact that his formulation achieved impact only at the cost of validity.
Consciousness is hardly lacking, as Hunter's definition
would imply it is, in aphasiacs, infants, and lower animals.

In spite of the persisting mood of behaviorism in psychological thought, still other efforts have been made to
deal with the question of 'consciousness.' It seems fair
to say, however, that none of these efforts has been any
more successful than the ones epitomized above. Cer-

tainly none has produced a formula which has achieved general acceptance. To review these additional attempts would thus seem to be unnecessary. It is clear that the problem of the definition of 'conscious experience' has remained unsolved.

This failure to arrive at an explicit delineation of 'consciousness' has been a rather sobering development. Perhaps discouraged by it, biologists and psychologists have tended to adopt a goal somewhat more modest than that of actual definition. They have appeared to be increasingly satisfied with the prospect of finding merely a "criterion of consciousness"—a behavioral sign which can be depended upon to reveal the presence of awareness. Obviously, this matter of a criterion of consciousness is intimately related to the central problem of the present chapter. Accordingly, it will be discussed at some length in the section which now follows.

The Emergence of a 'Criterion of Consciousness'

We may well begin the discussion with one of the most fascinating controversies in the whole history of science. It was the great argument which arose, during the nineteenth century, as to the existence of "spinal consciousness." The effects of that argument are still being felt: the modern debate about spinal conditioning, a debate summarized in the preceding chapter, has its roots in the earlier controversy (Shurrager and Culler 1940).

In his excellent summary of the dispute over spinal consciousness, Fearing (1930: 146–186) has described the impact upon early nineteenth-century physiology of the day's mounting evidence that the spinal cord was quite capable of mediating behavior of considerable complexity. This evidence naturally raised the question of just where in the nervous system consciousness might

reside. In 1853, E. Pflüger, the physiologist, published a
stirring and contentious answer to that question: Conscious experience was coextensive with *all* neural tissue.
In fact, said Pflüger, *"ein Kätzchen, dessen Dorsalmark
durchschnitten ist, zwei 'Seelen' bekommen hat"* (Fearing 1930: 162).

One of Pflüger's contemporaries, the physiologist-
philosopher R. H. Lotze, immediately took a stand in
strong opposition to that of Pflüger. Admitting that the
isolated spinal cord was indeed able to coordinate elaborate responses, Lotze nevertheless asserted that it did so
only insofar as earlier events had already established mechanical pathways within it. The spinal cord was thus regarded as operating entirely without benefit of consciousness, and the latter as existing within the brain
alone.

It was in such a fashion, then, that the controversy
over spinal consciousness was brought to a focus. It had
been in rather diffuse existence even before the exchange
between Pflüger and Lotze began; and it certainly remained alive long after that exchange ended, attracting
many participants and being endlessly confused by the
obscure semantics of nineteenth-century physiology. It
was also complicated by another factor: a great tendency
to seek new empirical evidence, even though the basic
issues were not empirical at all. As Fearing observes,
"There was little disagreement as to the *facts* regarding
the behavior of spinal animals as presented by Pflüger,
Goltz, Lewes, and others; their *theoretical interpretations*, however, were more varied" (Fearing 1930: 173;
italics added).

As time went by, it became clear that the dispute over
spinal consciousness could be settled only by prior agreement upon some basic criterion of consciousness. Hence,
several such criteria were proposed. They suffered dif-

fering fates. Two of the earliest suggestions, for example, were *movement* and *spontaneous movement;* but each was soon rejected. Not much attention was paid to *language* (a fact which reveals an interesting negative precedent for Hunter's later definition of 'consciousness' in terms of 'language response'). The general dimension of *coordination, adaptiveness,* or *purposefulness* was, on the other hand, taken rather seriously for a considerable period of time. As the implications of Darwinism began to be appreciated, however, even this notion lost its force. After all, natural selection might well be expected to produce unconscious reflexes which were biologically "purposeful."

In the wake of these several failures, there came, at the turn of the century, almost sudden apparent success. As early as 1885, Romanes had urged that *the ability to learn* was the true indicium of consciousness. This view had achieved but little prominence for a number of years. Now, however, it began to find firm espousal, particularly by Loeb, Bethe, and Sherrington (Fearing 1930: 174, 180; Washburn 1936: 1–32). Sherrington, in 1900, applied the test of learning ability specifically to the evidence for spinal consciousness, and flatly rejected the hypothesis that the latter existed (Fearing 1930: 174). Loeb was equally emphatic in 1903:

> The whole discussion of the "spinal-cord-soul" was needless, and might have been avoided if Pflüger had realized that those phenomena which the metaphysician calls consciousness are a function of the mechanism of associative memory. [Loeb, in Fearing 1930: 180]

There were no audible objections to these dicta, and the controversy over spinal awareness thus came to an abrupt end. That was an interesting fact in itself. More

important, however, was the fact that there had finally
emerged a plausible "criterion of consciousness": the capacity for learning.

The new criterion was rapidly and widely accepted. It
came to be invoked not merely in questions of spinal
consciousness but in every other area of organismic behavior as well. M. F. Washburn's widely used text, for
example, supported the general validity of this criterion
in each of its four editions (cf. Washburn 1936). R. M.
Yerkes tended to favor a multidimensional assessment of
degree of awareness, but he conceded, "If a single criterion is imperatively demanded we might agree to accept
rapidity of learning as a measure of the complexity of
the psychic" (Yerkes 1905: 147). Pavlov's application of
the technique of conditioning to problems of sensory acuity in animals gave additional impetus to the notion of
learning as an index of consciousness; and the learned
response became, during the first two or three decades of
the present century, the criterion of choice in the recognition of animal awareness. By 1935, Guthrie could remark securely that, to common sense, learning was the
sure indicator of the existence of mind (Guthrie 1935:
3).

It is not unfair to say that this is an attitude which has
survived and which is current today. To the degree that
there remains an interest in the sensory capacities of
lower animals, for example, there endures a confidence in
the learned response as an indicator of awareness. The
same confidence exists even when the problem is one of
demonstrating sensation in a human being: as is generally known, an individual who cannot be relied upon for a
verbal report may have his sensory acuity determined
through the use of the conditioned galvanic skin response. Thus, although there has been an unfortunate
lack of rigor about the whole matter, it continues to be
true that a stimulus to which a learned response can be

connected is generally regarded as one which evokes conscious experience.

It should now be clear, however, that the "lack of rigor about the whole matter" which has just been recognized has been not merely "unfortunate": *it has in fact been fatal.* For the preceding chapter has shown that the very notion of 'learning' depends fundamentally upon that of 'consciousness' itself; and it necessarily follows that, in order to establish the existence of learning in any given case, one must *first* demonstrate the presence of consciousness. Consciousness is the "criterion of learning." That being so, it is obvious that learning is not, and cannot be, the "criterion of consciousness."

The logic of this argument is so completely ineluctable that any amplification seems unnecessary. The very finality of the argument tends, however, to raise a new and rather insistent question. It is this: If the traditional criterion of consciousness is really so useless, why has it always *seemed* so useful? To that question, I wish now to propose an answer.

I should like to suggest that the scientist has seemed to find learning valuable as a criterion of consciousness only because *he has not required that learning itself be demonstrated in any objective way.* He has refused to intuit *sensation.* He has, however, been quite ready to intuit *learning;* and, once he has assumed the presence of learning, in any particular instance, he has been able to infer with logical impeccability the correlative presence of consciousness itself. In essence, the learning gambit has enabled the scientist to "prove" the existence of consciousness simply by presuming it.

An example of this mode of thought would be illuminating, and to find one is not difficult. We may, for instance, simply turn to the case of I. P. Pavlov.

As everyone knows, Pavlov regarded the establishment of any conditioned reflex as testimony to the existence of

sensory experience: learning having occurred, it was
accepted that the conditioned stimulus was arousing sensation. It should now be recognized, however, that the
phenomena which Pavlov was willing to regard as manifestations of a conditioned reflex, and thus of learning,
did not necessarily represent learning at all. Thus, for all
Pavlov knew: (1) the "unconditioned stimulus" might
well have been acting effectively only up to a neural level
below that of consciousness itself; (2) the impact of the
"conditioned stimulus" might well have been equally
modest; (3) the sort of mechanical connection that Pavlov himself envisaged might have been established at this
low level; and (4) without ever disturbing consciousness
at all, the "conditioned stimulus" might accordingly have
come to elicit the "conditioned response" in precisely the
fashion observed. Yet, in spite of such a distinct possibility to the contrary, Pavlov never hesitated in assuming
that he was in fact dealing with learning. The nature of
the stimuli involved, the general magnitude of the time
intervals, the complexity of the response, and (no doubt)
many other features of the experimental situation were
simply compelling to his intuition. From there on, the
whole thing was simple. If this *was* learning—that is, a
process involving conscious experience—then, manifestly, conscious experience was involved in this process.
More specifically, the "conditioned stimulus" was indeed
arousing sensation. *Q. E. D.*

Now, to explicate this mode of thought is not at all to
deride it. It has experienced a considerable degree of
pragmatic success, and it may well be defensible on
grounds of expediency alone. To explicate this mode of
thought is, however, to emphasize the basic nature of the
problem we now face. Not only do we lack any formal
statement of the meaning of 'conscious experience,' but
as we have just discovered, even our traditional 'criterion of consciousness' is completely deceitful. It is

thus evident that nothing at all resembling a serious definition of "conscious experience" is already in existence; and it is plain that, in attempting to develop an adequate characterization of the term, we shall have to begin at the most fundamental of levels.

The Definition of 'Conscious Experience'

The development of an adequate characterization of 'conscious experience' is, in fact, the responsibility of the present section of this essay. To discharge that responsibility, the section divides itself into two parts. The first of these evolves a formal definition; and the second tests that definition against intuitive conviction.

The Definition Proper. It will be remembered that, in Chapter I of the present volume, an "entirely commonplace," *ostensive* definition of 'conscious experience' was set forth. It typified 'conscious experience' (or "consciousness," or "awareness") by referring to "such phenomena as 'sensations,' 'perceptions,' 'thoughts,' 'images,' 'dreams,' 'wishes,' and 'emotions.'" It is at the level of this mere typification that 'conscious experience' and its synonyms have been used so far in the present book. Indeed, it is at such a level that they have always been used by mankind in general.

As may also be worth recalling, Chapter I emphasized the fact that all consciousness is simply a stream of events, that awareness is a process rather than an entity. It was further established in Chapter I that, as I believe, the stream of conscious events is utterly physical in nature. Finally, it was pointed out that the problem of rigorous definition still remained: even granting the premise that consciousness is a flux of purely physical events within the organism, precisely what kind of an event is it that is involved?

In seeking now to answer this question, we can reason-

ably use a method of successive approximations. We can
begin, that is, with an admittedly provisional formulation and go on to improve it gradually to the point of
acceptability. In this spirit, and recognizing that it is
basically the everyday notion of 'conscious experience'
with which we are now dealing, it is of some interest to
consider first of all how the question, "What is 'consciousness'?," might be answered offhand by ordinary
common sense.

The exact nature of the reply we might receive is, of
course, a matter for speculation. We may well begin,
however, by assuming that the answer would be completely unreflective. Thus, it might well, in essence, be
this: "Conscious experience is something happening inside us."

Although such an answer might seem valid enough for
a moment or two, it would soon strike even common sense
as grossly inadequate. After all, each of us possesses a
complex internal economy, busy all the time; and most of
this activity is not "consciousness" at all. Common sense
would thus be obliged to pause a bit. Having done so,
however, it would almost certainly make this decision:
"Consciousness," it would say, "is something happening
inside us that we can *talk about*."

Now, such a revision seems to limit the term 'conscious experience,' as it should be limited, to a greatly
restricted class of internal events. In reality, however, it
does not have this effect at all. As a moment of rumina-
tion will establish, we can actually "talk about" virtually
anything whatsoever that may be "happening inside us."
We are perfectly able, for example, to talk about a heart
murmur—once the physician has reported it to us. We
can readily discuss the functioning of our sudoriferous
glands—once we feel perspiration. And we can easily
report the onset of chemical activity in our own retinas
—once visual sensation is aroused. Yet, neither the heart

murmur, nor the glandular function, nor even the retinal activity constitutes "consciousness." It is clear that we must be much more explicit if we wish to have a valid definition.

The device that springs to mind at this point is that of adding some term like 'direct' or 'immediate' to our definition. Thus, it might well be amended to read as follows: "Consciousness is something happening inside us that we can talk about *directly*." To proceed in this fashion would indeed be to honor a hallowed tradition, inasmuch as consciousness has long been thought of as "direct experience" or "immediate experience." To proceed in this fashion would also, as a matter of fact, seem to be well advised. It will be necessary to move along rather cautiously, however. The meaning of 'directly' itself is not at all clear, and that word needs to be given sensible definition. Our status at the moment, then, is this: 'consciousness' is defined as 'something happening inside us that we can talk about directly'; but we require to be sure of the significance of 'directly.'

I think it will clarify matters for us now if we recall that any process which eventuates in "talking about" something actually consists of a long chain of physiological events. Characteristically, it involves a stimulated sense organ, an afferent neural impulse, a central process, an efferent discharge, and a muscular contraction. Only a portion of this sequence constitutes consciousness. Inasmuch, however, as one may "talk about" any event which even *results* in consciousness, one may now talk about the original stimulation to the sense organ, about the neural event to which that stimulation gives rise, about the next neural event in the sequence, and the next, and the next—and so on. In fact, artful stimulation at any point along this route could, in principle, reproduce the sequence of events from that point on, arouse consciousness, and permit verbal report.

Clearly, however, such "artful stimulation" could be an object of report only up to a certain point along the afferent-central-efferent pathway. An individual undergoing such stimulation could report it, we know, as its locus moved progressively up the afferent branch of the system. He could even report it as its locus became entirely central. As the point of stimulation continued to move, however, there would come a moment when it could no longer be "talked about." True, the stimulus might produce a forced vocalization—it might produce "talking": *but the stimulus could no longer be described or discussed.* As a matter of common intuition, we would agree, I believe, that the locus of stimulation had at this moment moved through and beyond the segment of the pathway whose function constituted consciousness. Consciousness, in fact, would be identified squarely with the *last* event in the afferent-central-efferent sequence that *could* be "talked about." *Consciousness*, therefore, *is something happening inside us that we can talk about directly—in the sense that it is the final event in the stimulus-response sequence that can be talked about.*

In this fashion, then, is the problem of the word 'directly' resolved. The term will be employed without further ado from now on. The definition in which the term has just appeared will, moreover, constitute a basis for further operations; and it will do no harm, at this point, to formalize it to a certain degree. What seems rather obviously indicated is a version of this kind: 'Consciousness' means 'an internal event about which one can talk directly.'

Now, formal or not, our successive approximations to the notion of 'consciousness' have embodied all along a persistent, serious flaw. In their dependence upon 'talk,' they have been sharply reminiscent of the approach suggested by W. S. Hunter; and Hunter's approach has already been assessed and found wanting. Lower animals do not talk at all, and neither do a great number of human beings. Many of these wordless organisms are, moreover, incapable of any other kind of symbolic "language response" (Hunter 1924). In spite of their complete failure to meet the criterion of speech, however, these organisms are plainly conscious.

A revision of our working definition, circumventing the problem of 'talk' but retaining the gist of the definition, is clearly required. Happily, it is not difficult to accomplish such a revision. We need only recognize that the element of speech is highly arbitrary, in any case. Thus, although it is true that one ordinarily reports a conscious experience orally, one could just as easily signal its existence by nodding his head or waving his hand. One can, in short, make any response he is asked to make, or any response he chooses to make, upon the occasion of a conscious experience. Our new rendition flows directly from these considerations. It is this: *'Consciousness'* is *'an internal event about which one can do, directly, whatever one wishes.'*

We are clearly remaining on a commonsense level, but we are also making headway with our task. We shall be able to make even further headway now by devoting our attention to the word 'can.'

In the context of the present definition, the word 'can' is susceptible of at least two different interpretations. The first of these interpretations, although natural and plausible, is entirely fallacious. Thus, to say that one *can* do what he wishes about an event is certainly to suggest strongly that, alternatively, one can *not* do what he wishes about the event. To accept this suggestion is, however, precisely the mistake. The simple fact of the matter is that it is totally impossible to *not* do what one wishes about any situation. It is true that the seeming experience of not doing what one wishes is commonplace; but this is indeed only a seeming experience. Thus, one may want intensely to respond to a certain situation in a certain way; and he may manage to "force himself" not to. Why does he "force himself," however, if not out of a competing wish? Clearly, he must want *to not* act more intensely than he wants *to* act. When he ends up by *not* acting, therefore, he is still "doing what he wants to do." He is simply not doing what he wanted to do in the first place.

It accordingly appears that 'can' is not to be construed here as 'may or may not.' Indeed, the second, less obvious, and really correct interpretation of 'can' is evidently something quite to the contrary. It is that, when one *can* do as one wishes, one necessarily *does* do as one wishes. The proper reading of 'can' is thus, flatly: 'can and does.' This circumstance is of manifest significance to our working definition of 'conscious experience.' A substitution of terms in the latter is now plainly called for. Making that substitution, we find that what we come out with is this: *'Conscious experience'* is *'an internal event about which one does do, directly, what one wants to do.'*

Although the progress we have made toward a final definition is not yet obvious, we are now in fact only one step from home.

The remaining great difficulty with our formulation is, of course, that it depends crucially upon the word 'want.' 'Want' is a term nearly as uncertain in meaning as 'conscious experience' itself, and to define the latter by recourse to the former is not very helpful. Our final requisite, therefore, is a satisfactory substitute for the phrase, 'what one wants to do.' Fortunately, such a substitute is not difficult to find.

Making our task comparatively easy is this fact: what one wants to do clearly depends upon what one expects in the way of consequences for any alternative course of action. What one wants to do, specifically, is that which will lead to a particular sort of consequence. Thus, if a certain conscious event has occurred repeatedly, and if differing consequences have attached to differing responses to this experience, one will now want to do the thing that has led to a restricted kind of consequence. If the situation changes systematically, and a new response becomes prerequisite to the same kind of consequence, one will soon "want" to make the new response.

It is our good fortune that, owing to the nature of the relationships just described, we need not talk in terms of 'wanting' at all. Thus, if conscious experience is indeed an internal event about which one does "what one wants to do," then it is necessarily an event about which one does *whatever happens to produce a certain set of circumstances*. In slightly more rigorous and coherent statement, we might say that *conscious experience* is *an internal event in direct response to which the organism does whatever produces a certain set of circumstances*: but even this rendition is not thoroughly satisfactory. What we need is a statement less dependent for its meaning upon the present context, and one more truly useful to an investigator actually prospecting for consciousness in a given organism. These requirements can be met, however; and, when they are, the statement that finally emerges is this: *'Conscious experience'* is *'an internal event to which an arbitrary response can be attached directly, by the process of following that response, when it occurs to that event, with a prespecified set of circumstances.'*

It is understood, of course, that 'response' itself is used in this final definition in its purely biological sense; used psychologically, it would beg the whole question of definition. 'Response' aside, however, the recognizably crucial terms in the formulation are 'arbitrary' and 'prespecified.' It is, in fact, precisely those two terms that convey the whole point of the definition—namely, that, in attempting to establish as conscious experience a given event within the organism, we may (1) select any one of several responses, (2) wait for that response to follow directly upon the event in question, and then (3) strengthen the connection between that event and that response by the immediate institution of a prechosen state of affairs; and, additionally, that we may at any time (4) select a *new* response, (5) shift the prechosen consequence to *its* support, and presently (6) have *it* (rather than the response first selected) directly attached to the crucial event. These things can be done, that is, *if, and only if, the event in question is indeed consciousness.*

Now, we seem to have achieved a definition, and it would appear to be a valid one. We have, nevertheless, once again arrived at a conclusion logically, only to find ourselves perhaps wishing that we could justify that conclusion somewhat more empirically. In short, it would be reassuring to know that the formulation achieved here was consonant with direct intuition.

To show that it is in fact so consonant happens to be entirely feasible. The strategy entailed is as follows: (1) Choose a situation, typical and representative of all such situations, in which genuine doubt exists as to the arousal of consciousness in a certain living object by a certain stimulus. (2) Envisage the application of that stimulus to that object, within each of a number of differing matrices of accompanying events. (3) Identify the particular kind of matrix which leads to the intuitive supposition that consciousness has been aroused. (4) Show that, granting just the same sort of context, the formal definition of 'conscious experience' also points to the presence of awareness. And finally: (5) Note that the nature of the situation originally chosen permits generalization of the congruence thus demonstrated.

In the paragraphs which follow, the strategy just now outlined is put into effect.

A Supporting Case. The first step must be the choosing of an instance. That instance may be either real or imaginary. Such latitude is permissible because the procedure now contemplated is simply that of comparing two decisions as to the suitability of the term 'conscious experience': the decision prompted by common intuition, and the one specified by the definition at hand. Obviously, the two decisions must be made with respect to a common case; but the case itself may equally well be either factual or hypothetical. This is a situation of which I should actually like to take advantage; that is to say, the instance I wish to nominate (although it has been suggested by one of the real issues mentioned earlier in the present chapter) is indeed a hypothetical one. It has to do with the question of spinal consciousness.

Let us envisage, then, a modern investigator who, for reasons of his own, wishes to reopen the question of awareness in the spinal cord. His experimental animal happens to be the dog. The investigator has, however, wished to be perfectly certain that he is working with an unequivocally spinal subject, and he has also wished to be constantly aware of the fact that he is doing so. He has therefore, with great technical skill, dissected away and removed the animal's head and forequarters. The actual preparation accordingly consists simply of the caudal thorax, the abdomen, and the hindquarters. Ingeniously maintained by a mechanically circulated supply of blood, this preparation is suspended in a sort of hammock, with the two legs swinging free below. To the tail is affixed an electrical connection through which the experimenter is able to administer a mild shock; and the basic question in the experimenter's mind is whether or not the preparation can truly feel such a shock.

There is, in fact, an initial suggestion that the preparation can. The investigator discovers immediately that, when the electrical stimulus is administered, a diffuse muscular twitching is engendered. The twitching is slight and momentary; but it is undeniable. Thus, the preparation is at least *reacting* to the onset of the shock. The investigator is encouraged by this finding, but he is quick to recognize its equivocality. Perhaps the electrical current is merely stimulating the muscles of the preparation by direct conduction; or perhaps, although the stimulus may indeed be activating neural circuits into and out of the spinal cord, these circuits are purely reflexive in nature. Obviously, there is as yet no proof of spinal sensation.

Obviously, too, some elaboration of procedure is called for; and it is natural that the experimenter should now begin to think in terms of replicating the phenomenon of "spinal conditioning." Let us imagine that he does indeed think in this fashion, and that he actually goes ahead with the task of replication.

A prerequisite to this task is the provision of a new electrical connection, this one to the right hand leg of the experimental preparation. This provision having been made, however, the investigator embarks upon the conditioning procedure itself. He runs a series of trials in which a slight shock to the tail just precedes an intense shock to the leg. During each of the first few of these trials, the leg flexes appreciably only as the intense shock is applied directly to the leg itself. After a number of pairings of the two stimuli, however, the mild shock to the tail begins to elicit a discernible preliminary flexion of the leg. Shortly, the leg is flexing vigorously immediately upon administration of the stimulus to the tail, and clearly before the shock is applied to the leg itself. It appears to the experimenter that he has elicited the signs of "spinal conditioning."

Contemplating the headless and radically reduced experimental preparation with which he has been working, the investigator ponders the meaning of these signs. The preparation inspires no intuitive conviction whatsoever that it harbors awareness; and, freed by this fact from a possible initial bias, the investigator now sees little need to postulate the existence of consciousness in order to explain his findings. At the most, he has shown simply that an originally ineffectual stimulus, paired often enough with a vigorous motor response, eventually comes to elicit the latter of its own accord. Such a phenomenon might easily represent several events far less imposing than actual consciousness. It might, for instance, mirror a kind of "neurobiotaxis"—a tendency for contiguously active neural systems gradually to make junction. The investigator thus discounts the possibility of conscious experience in his preparation. Intuitively aware, furthermore, that "conditioning" actually depends upon "consciousness," he also rejects the notion that he has demonstrated spinal conditioning. We must agree with him, I think, in all of these conclusions.

It is apparent to our hypothetical investigator that his procedures must undergo still further evolution; and, having tried the technique of "classical conditioning," he is now strongly inclined toward that of "instrumental conditioning." He decides, in fact, to employ the device of instrumental conditioning in an attempt to reverse the present "conditioned" response completely. He sets out to attach to the stimulus to the tail not the *flexion*, but the *extension* of the right hand leg.

The experimenter returns to his preparation and makes two changes in its status. First, he removes the electrical connection from the right leg, leaving both legs once again free of any encumbrance. Second, he shaves the hair from a circular area, about three inches in diameter, on the right hip; and to this area he cements a small electrical device which, when it is activated, gently massages the skin beneath. In this act, he is prompted by the thought that the sort of tactual stimulation which seems to be rewarding to the whole animal may also prove positively reinforcing to the abbreviated preparation with which he is working.

His simple instrumentation having been accomplished, the experimenter now sets out to "extinguish" the existing response to the shock on the tail. Extinction is accomplished in a fairly long series of trials. Each trial consists merely of the administration of the stimulus to the tail, with no other stimulus being applied. During the first several trials, the established response of leg flexion occurs vigorously. As the series is extended, however, that response grows less and less pronounced. Ultimately, the stimulus to the tail is followed by no systematic reaction at all. Extinction is thus complete.

The investigator now puts his new plan into effect. The shock to the tail is continued, trial by trial; but the activation of the stimulator mounted upon the hip is made contingent on the nature of whatever small response happens to follow that shock. If response is totally lacking, or if it consists in a *flexion* of the right leg, the stimulator is not energized. If, however, the response consists in even a rudimentary *extension* of the leg, the stimulator is turned on, and the hip of the preparation is stroked mechanically for a period of five seconds. It is the experimenter's private opinion that nothing will come of this procedure, which strikes him, when he thinks about it, as being a little silly. He feels, nevertheless, that it is at least worth trying.

As a matter of fact, the actual result completely confounds the investigator's expectation; for the extensional response is, in fact, eventually established. It is true that this result is achieved only at the cost of long, patient effort. Thus, several trials are required before even the first, slight extension occurs—to be succeeded immediately, of course, by five seconds of mechanical stimulation. Another series of unproductive trials then follows, before a second critical response occurs and is similarly reinforced. And so it goes. As time passes, however, the response of extension occurs more and more frequently and with increasing definition. Finally, it is both strong and dependable.

The investigator is understandably captivated by this improbable development, but he is also thoroughly aware of the need for some kind of check upon it. It occurs to him that such a check might be provided by an attempt to reverse the preparation's response once more, an effort to restore the original *flexion* of the leg as the reaction to the shock to the tail. Accordingly, he sets out to produce, if possible, just such a reversal.

The experimental trials are consequently resumed, but now under still another policy. Now the stimulator is activated only upon a discernible *flexion* of the right hand leg, with any other reaction whatsoever remaining unreinforced. Once again, of course, the trials repeat themselves almost interminably. Eventually, however, the same sort of history which resulted earlier in the stable response of extension does result now in the stable response of flexion: when the electrical stimulus is applied to the tail, the predictable result is a prompt and definite retraction of the leg.

At this point, the investigator ends his program of stimulation. Having been quite unprepared for the outcome of his attempt at "instrumental conditioning," he now contemplates that outcome in some amazement. His first thought, naturally enough, is that his results ought to be confirmed many times over; somehow, they may be artifactitious. If they are not, however, what then? What if one thoroughly competent repetition after another, in one laboratory after another, should substantiate his findings beyond any reasonable doubt?

After giving full consideration to this question, the investigator is forced to admit that, then, he would have to concede sentience to the spinal cord. He would be steadfast in regarding the behavior in question as a simple reflection of underlying neural events. At the same time, however, he would feel that those neural events must include among them one event of the particular kind called "sensation." Only by assuming that the shock to the tail was in truth being *felt* could the experimenter account for the existence of such a strikingly adaptive response to that shock. He reminds himself now that, earlier, he had considered accepting the premise of sensation, merely on the basis of his demonstration of "classical conditioning"—a comparatively simple phenomenon. He had refrained from actually doing so, in the conviction that he should require, as his indicium, behavior of a more complex nature. He is now exploring the implications of a form of behavior which is in its essence as complex as behavior ever gets. He could hardly avoid ascribing awareness to the neural centers which might mediate it.

It is here submitted that, when our hypothetical investigator thinks in this fashion, he thinks for all of us. Faced with his problems and depending, as he has depended, upon common intuition, we would surely arrive at the same decision he has. We would not, that is, accept a manifestation of "classical conditioning" as evidence of conscious experience in the spinal cord; but we would find ourselves strongly persuaded by unmistakable "instrumental conditioning."

It remains only to be pointed out, then, that such a persuasion would be entirely consonant with the formal definition here under scrutiny. Thus, the stimulus to the tail of the imaginary preparation would be regarded intuitively as arousing sensation: and it is that stimulus also which would clearly be producing an internal event to which an arbitrary response (flexion or extension of the leg) could be directly attached by the procedure of following that response with a predetermined consequence (the mechanical stimulation). In this correspondence between intuition and deductive abstraction we find, of course, a measure of support for the definition here espoused.

To be stressed now, in taking leave of our hypothetical case, is the fact that the "measure of support" it provides is actually rather considerable. It was chosen as an instance embodying the essential features, and only the essential features, of any situation in which the presence of conscious experience is problematical. Supposedly, therefore, the agreement between definition and intuition which has been found in connection with this one instance could be demonstrated in connection with any number of other instances, also. A single example thus serves to uphold the proposed definition not only once but a great many times.

A Final Note on the Definition of 'Consciousness' and 'Awareness.' It would appear now that we have arrived at an adequate verbalization of the concept of 'conscious experience,' basing that verbalization upon the general idea of the stream of sensation, perception, thought, and the like. Throughout, the terms 'consciousness' and 'awareness' have been equated fully with 'conscious experience' itself. This usage is really completely orthodox, and 'consciousness' and 'awareness' in this sense thus acquire, as their own, precisely the definition of 'conscious experience' which has been abstracted above.

To be noted now, however, is the fact that 'consciousness' and 'awareness' are often employed, without qualification, in a single highly specialized sense: that of 'insight' or 'understanding' or 'recognition of relationships.' Good examples of this second usage are abundantly available in Freudian discourse. An "unconscious motive," for instance, is not a motive aroused by nonconscious experience; it does not lead to action of which the individual is unaware; it is not even necessarily a motive unfelt: it is simply a motive which is not understood. An even better example can be found in connection with the contemporary interest in "learning without awareness." As Kimble has well pointed out:

> . . . someone is sure to protest that this [i.e., the distinction between being awake and being asleep] isn't exactly what is meant by the term awareness in discussions of learning without awareness. If one asks what *is* meant, the forthcoming answer is . . . that what is involved is the recognition (or lack of it) *in subjects who are fully aware* of certain features of the experimental situation. . . . In effect the question is whether subject must be aware of the relationship which, on other grounds, we know to be necessary for learning to occur. [Kimble 1962: 29–30; italics added]

It would not be very difficult, I imagine, to formulate a definition appropriate to this second sense of 'consciousness' and 'awareness.' To do so is not a present goal, however. The words have been defined here, and are used here, simply with the force of 'conscious experience.'

Summary and Conclusion

The present chapter has attempted to examine and to verbalize the concept of 'conscious experience.'

It began by noting that earlier efforts to formalize the concept have been ineffective. It then went on to consider the criterion of consciousness which has developed historically as a substitute for actual definition. That criterion —the attachment, to a stimulus, of a learned response— was shown to be quite illusory: the demonstration of learning depends basically upon the establishment of consciousness itself.

In the main section of the paper, the meaning of 'conscious experience' was sought in an analysis of the everyday, universal usage of the term. A definition was reached. It was tested against intuitive judgment, through the presentation of the account of an hypothetical, yet prototypical, experiment. The definition appeared to dictate a sensible conclusion in this pragmatic test, and it was accordingly submitted as generally valid. It goes as follows: *'Conscious experience'* is *'an internal event to which an arbitrary response can be attached directly, by the process of following that response, when it occurs to that event, with a prespecified set of circumstances.'*

In conclusion, it remains to be emphasized here that (at least as I believe) this, and nothing more or less than this, is precisely what we mean when we talk about 'conscious experience.' The suggested definition does not specify merely a "criterion of consciousness." It is not just "one way of looking at the problem of awareness." It is, unless I am mistaken, a verbalization which can always be substituted with utter fidelity for 'conscious experience' whenever the latter term is used in its customary sense.

Inasmuch as the other basic notions in biology and psychology depend importantly upon 'consciousness,' this definition has certain systematic implications. These implications will not be pursued here. Rather, they will be considered as seems appropriate in the next chapter. That chapter will be the final essay in this volume, and it will attempt a summary integration of all that has now been said.

REFERENCES

Fearing, F. 1930. *Reflex Action*. Williams and Wilkins, Baltimore.

Guthrie, E. R. 1935. *The Psychology of Learning*. Harper, New York and London.

Holt, E. B. 1914. *The Concept of Consciousness*. Macmillan, New York.

Hunter, W. S. 1924. "The Problem of Consciousness." *Psychol. Rev., 31*, 1–31.

Kimble, G. A. 1962. "Classical Conditioning and the Problem of Awareness." In: Eriksen, C. W. (ed.) ; *Behavior and Awareness: A Symposium of Research and Interpretation*; Duke University Press, Durham, N.C.

Lashley, K. S. 1923. "The Behavioristic Interpretation of Consciousness: I and II." *Psychol. Rev., 30*, 237–272 and 329–353.

Lashley, K. S. 1958. "Cerebral Organization and Behavior." In: Solomon, H. C., S. Cobb, and W. Penfield, (eds.) ; 1958; *The Brain and Human Behavior: Volume 36, Research Publications of the Association for Research in Nervous and Mental Disease;* Williams and Wilkins, Baltimore. Also, reprinted in: Beach, F. A., D. O. Hebb, C. T. Morgan, and H. W. Nissen, (eds.) ; 1960; *The Neuropsychology of Lashley* (pp. 529–543) ; McGraw-Hill, New York.

Perry, R. B. 1904. "Conceptions and Misconceptions of Consciousness." *Psychol. Rev., 11*, 282–296.

Shurrager, P. S., and E. Culler. 1940. "Conditioning in the Spinal Dog." *J. Exper. Psychol., 26*, 133–159.

Tolman, E. C. 1927. "A Behavioristic Definition of Consciousness." *Psychol. Rev., 34*, 433–439.

Washburn, M. F. 1936. *The Animal Mind*. Macmillan, New York.

Yerkes, R. M. 1905. "Animal Psychology and Criteria of the Psychic." *J. Philos., Psychol. and Scientific Methods, 2*, 141–149.

NOTE

A briefer version of this paper was presented to the Psychology Colloquium of Wake Forest University, in 1964.

VI

IMPLICATIONS

THE CONCEPTUAL analysis undertaken by the present volume has now been completed. Out of that analysis, certain tentative insights seem to have emerged.

Among those insights is the realization that the word 'stimulus' has two meanings. The first meaning, extant among biologists, is the more general; the second, peculiar to psychologists, is the more restricted. The word 'response' also has both a general, biological significance, and a restricted, psychological one. Especially interesting is the fact that, in the case of each of the terms 'stimulus' and 'response,' the distinction between the biological meaning and the psychological meaning depends fundamentally upon the idea of 'conscious experience.' Nor is that all; for it develops further that the notion of 'learning,' too, depends crucially upon that of 'conscious experience.' 'Conscious experience' itself thus emerges as a decidedly basic term, requiring a formal definition which eschews any other term logically dependent upon it.

Now, the situation so described appears to have a number of implications. It suggests, for one thing, that the essential relationship between biology and psychology has not so far been clearly visualized; indeed, it suggests that the nature of psychology itself, as a scientific enterprise, has not been entirely understood. Moreover, it prompts the thought that the methods now used in psychological research might not be optimal—that there might be real prospects for their improvement.

Such implications seem to merit exploration. They will accordingly be considered in the two sections which now follow: "Psychology as a Biological Science" and "Methodological Possibilities." A brief third section will provide a summary; the present chapter, and this monograph, will thereupon come to a close.

Psychology as a Biological Science

The thought that psychology is a biological science is, of course, not new. Especially in North America, psychology has long regarded itself as being intimately related to biology proper. It is truly doubtful, however, that either of those sciences has ever seen itself as related to the other in the fashion indicated by their respective definitions of 'stimulus' and 'response.'

As will be recalled, the biologist regards as a response any release of chemical energy by a living object; but the psychologist's "response" is the particular sort of biological response which is prompted by conscious experience. Similarly, the biologist sees any event, within or upon a living object, which is of consequence only insofar as it produces a response, as a stimulus; but the psychologist recognizes as "stimuli" only those biological stimuli which produce the specific response of consciousness. It is true that the logical consequences of this definitional situation are not entirely clear-cut: it is obvious that the psychologist is limiting himself to one realm of biology, but it does not necessarily follow that the biologist is abdicating that realm to him entirely. It is plain enough, nevertheless, that biology and psychology have established some sort of division of labor in terms of consciousness; and it would seem worthwhile to try to understand that arrangement better.

The nature of the relationship between psychology and biology can perhaps be brought into clearest focus by recalling the origins of psychology as a science. What the first scientific psychologists actually did, then, was to engage in careful introspection, reporting in detail upon the various states of awareness produced by rather simple stimuli. Their introspective reports were, of course, immediately turned to the use of the biology of the time. Here was a new way to study the functioning of the organism!

Now, however: In what terms did the introspectionist describe his own conscious experience? Certainly not in terms of the chemical changes and the transformations of energy which actually went to make it up. Even had it occurred to him that consciousness might be literally physical, he would have been no more able than anyone else to render such a description. *He was forced, in essence, to describe each experience as being the kind of experience normally aroused in him by a certain sort of stimulus* (cf. Attneave 1962: 628; Smart 1963: 94–95). When he reported an experience of blueness, he was (no matter what circumstances might actually have been prompting that experience) really saying, "In my brain, there is occurring an event of the sort usually instigated by visual stimulation at 475 millimicra." When he reported a sound's becoming louder, he was similarly saying, "In my brain, there is occurring a physical change of the sort usually produced by an increase in the amplitude of an acoustic stimulus." And so on; for what else, indeed, can words like 'blue' and 'loud' possibly mean?

We thus see that, whatever they may have thought they were doing, the first psychologists were in fact describing the physical states of their own brains. They were investigating the nature of consciousness in a way which was truly biological. They were, however, using a method which was macroscopic in the extreme: that of specifying the various sorts of conscious events merely in terms of the stimulus situations which normally instigated them.

Historically speaking, the introspective method did not for very long constitute the only avenue of psychological research. Introspection endured, but psychology soon turned to objective techniques, also. In particular, the investigation of animal behavior began to flourish. Noteworthy in this connection is the fact that conscious experience, as specified by its customary stimulus, remained the topic of focal interest (cf. Boring 1932: 33). The experimental animals were wide awake, and the stimuli to which they were exposed were calculated to arouse sensation. Research addressed itself, in effect, to such questions as, "What stimuli seem to produce any sensation at all?" and, "By how much do two stimuli need to differ before they appear to produce two sensations sufficiently disparate to command disparate responses?" Now, too, the effects, as well as the causes, of consciousness came under scrutiny: "If an animal undergoes a given conscious experience—as defined by the effective stimulus situation—what does he do?" Or, more importantly, "If an animal experiences some *combination* of conscious events (specified, again, in terms of their respective stimuli), how is his behavior modified?" It is clear that, introspective or not, psychology had defined itself as *the science of the nature, causes, and effects of conscious experience—conscious experience being specified always in terms of the stimulus situations instigating it.*

I wish to submit that psychology has continued to define itself in this fashion. Introspection has gone out of style, but the temper of modern psychology remains that of the formulation just cited. It is this fact that accounts for the systematic difference between the psychologist's concepts of 'stimulus' and 'response' and those of the biologist. It is this fact that explains the psychologist's isolation of the phenomenon of learning, envisaged as he envisages it, and his enormous interest in that phenomenon. It is this fact that underlies the constant smuggling of introspective data into what is conventionally described as "the science of behavior." Consciousness, specified by reference to the stimulus, is the touchstone of what is psychological.

Perhaps that point, unexpected though it may have been, can be granted. We return, then, to the original question: What is the precise nature of the relationship of psychology to biology?

The foregoing sketch has already provided a tentative answer to that question, of course, for it has portrayed psychology simply as one domain of biology broadly conceived. Such a portrayal appears to be valid in essence. In pragmatic detail, however, the relationship is really not quite so simple. That is to say, the domain of psychology is in point of fact a rather highly autonomous one. It has developed its own concepts, techniques, and insights, many of them well removed from the realm of the microtome and centrifuge. It is not a province into which even the biologist can stroll casually, with any hope of successful sojourn. For all practical purposes, biology and psychology have thus become separate sciences.

Separate though they may be, biology and psychology nevertheless clearly share some kind of kinship; and the task of delineating that kinship remains. We may accordingly note with interest that the relationship between the two sciences is often compared to the one that obtains between physics and chemistry. Unfortunately, the comparison as it is usually drawn is somewhat inexact. It pictures psychology as a sort of macroscopic general biology, and this picture is not entirely valid. A psychologist does not necessarily become a biologist when he resorts to microelectrodes, and a biologist does not necessarily become a psychologist when he turns to the gross observation of living things. Perhaps, however, the comparison can be sharpened up now to the point at which it will become genuinely useful.

It is true enough then that both physics and chemistry share an interest in the entire world of substance. It is further true that the physicist's approach to this world is microscopic in the extreme, and the chemist's comparatively gross. Analogously, biology and psychology share an interest, not really in all aspects of life, but actually in the nature, causes, and effects of conscious experience in particular. To the biologist, the problem of consciousness is simply one of the many presented by the living objects with which he deals; and he would expect to attack it by means of his usual techniques of cytology, histology, physiology, and biochemistry. To the psychologist, the problem is obviously central; and he would expect to attack it at the comparatively molar level already described. Like physics and chemistry, therefore, biology and psychology do indeed share a common topic. That topic is consciousness; biology approaches it microscopically, and psychology approaches it macroscopically.

In the end, as we know, psychology reduces to biology. It is surprising how frequently psychologists become perturbed over this connection between the two disciplines and feel threatened by it. When biology and psychology have finally achieved complete success, they realize, any psychological principle, problem, or phenomenon whatsoever will be reducible to physiological terms. But, they ask, will the laws of psychology not then become superfluous, and the science and technology of psychology not evaporate? Would it not in fact be reasonable to begin to save time and effort immediately by abandoning psychology as a formal discipline and concentrating directly upon research at the purely physiological level?

Surely such anxiety is unwarranted. Chemistry reduces to physics, too; and the laws of chemistry are (or someday will be) totally explicable in terms of the laws of physics. This circumstance, however, has never tempted anyone to advocate the abolition of chemistry as a science. In numberless practical situations, the problems of physical matter can be approached and solved more effectively in terms of the laws of chemistry than they can in terms of the laws of physics—even though the latter are indeed the more basic, and even though they are in principle perfectly applicable. The macroscopic viewpoint has obviously had its own advantages in this situation at least.

It seems entirely probable that the macroscopic viewpoint will also endow psychology, into the indefinite future, with its own particular advantages. Just as there are situations in which the laws of chemistry are more useful than those of physics, so there will continue to be situations in which the principles of psychology are more useful than those of biology. Even, for example, when we can say that a given peculiarity in an individual's behavior reflects a state of hyperconductivity in synapses number 7,638,491 through 10,821,460, it will still be more convenient to reduce the conductivity of those synapses by psychotherapy than to do so by surgery or medication; and psychotherapy must proceed in terms of psychological principles. Without a doubt, this same sort of logic will continue to apply not only in the fields of therapy, counseling, and guidance, but in such vast additional areas as training, education, attitude formation, and so on.

In more general statement, the foregoing argument obviously becomes the rationale of the pyramid of the sciences. Nature is a unity, but there is profit in approaching it now on one level of complexity and now on another. Within this schema, psychology, as well as biology, manifestly has an enduring value.

Methodological Possibilities

If the foregoing section has been essentially sound in its argument—if consciousness is indeed "the touchstone of what is psychological"—then psychology today finds itself in a posture that is evidently grotesque. For, in spite of the central importance of conscious experience to even modern psychology, the latter institution seems determined to have as little to do with the former phenomenon as it possibly can.

It is interesting that both Lashley (1958) and Feigl (1959) have drawn a parallel between psychology's mode of coping with the problem of awareness and the Freudian mechanism of repression. There would seem to be some justice in that comparison. Both Lashley and Feigl have alluded, moreover, to the unhealthy character of repression; and there is, in the behavioristic literature, clear evidence of pathological hypersensitivity. In another segment of the literature, too, there are now signs of an explosive abreaction. During just the past few years, there has burgeoned within psychology a kind of a neomentalism (e.g., May 1961; MacLeod 1964; Rogers 1964; May 1967; Giorgi 1967). Under such names as 'humanistic psychology,' 'existential psychology,' and 'phenomenology,' it has advocated an intuitive, uncritical, undisciplined sort of introspectionism which is bound to end up in a welter of futility (cf. Koch 1964, esp. 34–38). The abreaction thus promises to be as unfortunate as the repression itself.

The basic mischief, the emotional denial of the importance of awareness, was, of course, done a half century ago. Its circumstances are widely known, and there is no need to review them here. What might be emphasized here, however, is the genuine absurdity of the original behavioristic flight from consciousness and introspection. For one thing, it took place very largely in a miasma of

psychophysical parallelism; hence, conscious experience
was gratuitously—and mistakenly—assumed to be eter-
nally private. Furthermore, the behavioristic attitude toward introspective report was completely at odds with
the behavioristic doctrine of reliance upon sense data:
perceptions, thoughts, and emotions were never to be
reported; but perceptions, thoughts, and emotions were
at the same time regarded as muscular events—and their
description would therefore have been just as "sensory"
as the description of the behavior of an animal in a maze.

Even at the start, there were those who saw defensible
alternatives to the flight from consciousness. In 1922, for
instance, M. F. Washburn was urging "introspection as
an objective method" (Washburn 1922). Recent years
also have provided responsible opposition, of varying de-
grees of vigor, to the disallowance of introspective report
(e.g., Carnap 1956: 70–71; Zener 1958; Burt 1962;
Homme 1965). There has thus arisen the feeling that the
kind of psychology that draws its data entirely from
gross observation is doomed to superficiality and hence to
failure. It is asserted that what is urgently required is a
mode of observation which gains access to the most central phases of the stimulus-response sequence. Given the
kind of data such a mode of observation would provide, it
is said, psychology might have some chance for success.

I believe it is clear that the present series of essays
tends to reinforce such a responsible plea for the read-
mission of introspective evidence to court. It does so
mainly, perhaps, through its arguments in support of
physical monism. The principal objection to the report of
"states of awareness" has always been that those states
were qualitatively different from physical events, and
thus by their basic nature utterly beyond observation by
anyone other than their owner. That objection dissipates
in the face of physical monism; for it follows from the
latter view that awareness, being part of the material

world itself, is in principle entirely public. It is true that
it is just now technically impractical to observe someone
else's consciousness. It is worth remarking, however, that
it is often quite impractical to observe someone else's
rats, too. The two cases are in essence quite equivalent.

The present analysis tends to support the case of introspection in a second way, also. Heretofore, the term 'conscious experience' has stood without formal definition,
as did the word "life" for so long. The result in both cases
seems to have been much the same—namely, the encour-
agement of a certain mystique about the phenomenon
signified by the term (Smith 1951, 1958b). Chapter V
has now provided a definition for "conscious experience."
That definition may or may not be entirely satisfactory.
At the very least, however, it constitutes a distinct improvement upon the vacuum it replaces. To the extent
that it may succeed in dispelling the aura of inaccessibil-
ity surrounding consciousness, it may encourage a serious approach to that phenomenon; and such an approach
might well entail introspective report.

I wish, then, to urge the legitimacy and the utility of
introspection. I hasten to say immediately, though, just
what kind of introspection I mean, because the opportu-
nities for misunderstanding are so appallingly numerous. The particular sort of introspective technique I have
in mind is in fact one which would be purely descriptive,
empirical, and factual. It would simply report upon the
flow of sensation, perception, image, thought, and impulse. It would provide a species of data upon internal
behavior exactly comparable to that arising from the
usual observation of external behavior. Indeed, matters
could easily be arranged so that the two kinds of information would complement one another rather precisely.

The kind of introspection I do *not* have in mind is the
kind which assumes that access to inner events somehow
confers a prescience about their causation. As was em-

phasized most strongly in Chapter I, even awareness is merely a sequence of events; it is just as much a stimulus-response phenomenon as is overt conduct. Whether we observe outer behavior, inner behavior, or the interflow of the two, we deal only with discrete happenings. The process of drawing conclusions as to cause and effect on the basis of *inner* events is every bit as precarious as the corresponding process carried on in terms of *outer* events. Introspection gives us no privileged knowledge whatsoever as to "why we do things."

The methodology thus proposed might perhaps be regarded as a kind of introspectional behaviorism. "Behaviorism," because it recognizes that the basic data with which psychology must deal are always stimulus-response data—either the stimulus-response data of overt, explicit behavior, or the stimulus-response data of covert, implicit behavior. "Introspectional," because it is willing to honor the reports of competent observers, made under acceptable conditions of observation, as to inner events as well as outer. It neither flees in terror from introspection nor rushes to embrace it as a self-validating source of absolute truth. It merely makes what seems to be the reasonable suggestion that a new and important class of data be exploited to the degree that it can be depended upon.

Now the present discussion of methodological possibilities might well be brought to a close at this point, and perhaps it should be. It has rested upon a minimum of substantive premises, and its conclusions therefore possess a considerable degree of generality. As it happens, however, the picture it has drawn becomes especially meaningful and understandable if it can be placed within the framework of one additional assumption: the assumption that the "motor theory of consciousness" is in fact true. I should like to make precisely that assumption now and to explore its consequences. The question as to its legitimacy can and will be faced somewhat later in the present paper.

The motor theory of consciousness is in fact described, although it is not actually espoused, in Chapter I of this volume. The earlier description is rather brief, and it is written only in the broad terms which were necessary at that point in the exposition. Accordingly, it seems appropriate now to review in greater detail just what the motor theory of consciousness has to say, specifically within the context of physical monism, about a typical sequence of behavior. Such a review is undertaken below.

Commonly, then, a behavioral sequence is initiated when a stimulus impinges upon a receptor. The receptor so activated prompts in turn a burst of neural impulses, which pass along a connecting afferent pathway and into a sensory-projection area of the brain. Here sensation occurs.

Inasmuch as sensation is a completely physical event, it can and does cause other physical events. In this case, it initiates further neural impulses. The impulses course now along associational pathways. The particular route they follow may have been established by sheer maturation. More likely, in an organism of any age, it has been formed to some degree—and can likewise be re-formed —by the purely physical process we call 'learning.' Be that as it may, this fact remains: the functioning of the associational pathways is in itself unconscious; there is no state of awareness, no conscious experience at all, connected with their activity.

Associational pathways lead ultimately to motor projection areas; and associational impulses thus finally evoke motor impulses. Running along efferent pathways, those motor impulses reach an assortment of muscle fibers. Impulses cross myoneural junctions, the principles of muscular physiology assert themselves, and a pattern of contraction is produced. There has, however, still been no conscious experience beyond that of the original sensation.

It is quite possible that the behavior so generated is an overt, palpable response. Perhaps the behaving individual has succeeded in dodging a flying object of some kind, for example. In such a case, the muscular activity itself inevitably becomes a new stimulus. Receptors of several varieties, in muscles, tendons, and joints, respond to the pattern of contraction. New afferent impulses course to the somesthetic projection area, and now new sensation finally arises.

It is equally likely, however, that the behavior in question is an act of perception. Thus, it is not a gross commitment to action; rather, it is a tentative, covert "identifying response" (Gibson and Gibson 1950). It is the sort of mediating response that has been learned by the organism because of its utility to him in his dealings with the environment. This perceptual response in itself is naturally quite outside of awareness. It "reaches consciousness" in essentially the same fashion as a more overt response might have: it stimulates receptors within the muscles, the receptors initiate afferent impulses, and the latter produce their own pattern of sensation. Such a pattern now becomes the afferent basis for new associational activity, new efferent outflow, and new behavior.

It will perhaps be sufficient merely to suggest what forms this new behavior might take. Again, obviously, it might consist of an overt, public response: a reaching out to push aside a tree branch, a vocalized greeting to a friend. It might be a "thought" or an "image": a further covert, representational motor response, again appreciated in consciousness only by virtue of afferent return from the muscles involved. It might, finally, represent the beginning of an overt action: an "impulse" or "wish"; and, if the impulse to action happened to be strong but somewhat disorganized, the behavior might be

regarded as an "emotion" (Smith 1958a). To be noted
once more is the fact that "wishes" (like any of the
other behavioral phenomena mentioned) are completely
determined and completely inevitable—as we know them
to be by common experience; and the further fact the
individual is in no way constrained from carrying out
whatever wishes he may have.

It is transparent, in the foregoing account, that the
cycle of events with which psychology must always deal
is that of stimulus, sensation, and response. All "conscious phenomena" reduce to mosaics of sensation, as,
indeed, competent introspection strongly implies they
should. Although the study of sensation proper would
seem to constitute a perfectly appropriate activity for
psychology to pursue, it is still true that a preoccupation
with sense experience *per se* is not today a major focus of
psychological endeavor, nor is it likely to become so in the
future. What is much more generally interesting, and
probably much more generally important, is the dynam-
ics of behavior: the chain of stimulus and response, in
which sensation is a necessary but essentially passive
link.

If the flux of stimulus and response is indeed to be
studied, then what the motor theory suggests first of all
is that it be studied quite externally. Not only gross
behavior; but images, thoughts, perceptions, and wishes
become, in the view of the motor theorist, "overt." An
outside observer, using sufficiently advanced instrumentation, could recognize behavior of the latter sort as well
as the former. Recognizing it, he could place it as the
response to a preceding stimulus, and as the stimulus to a
succeeding response. The description of behavioral events
would thus be greatly enriched and manifestly enhanced
in utility.

The millenial picture thus created disappears, however, upon second thought. All that has been described

may well be feasible in principle, but it is beyond any hope of attainment in practice. There would be required a fantastically elaborate system of sensors interfusing the muscular system, of integrating computers to handle the sensors' input, and of annunciational devices to deliver the final output. What would be required, in fact, would be something closely resembling the somesthetic pathways, the brain, and the neuromotor system. And thus, of course, arises the obvious thought: inasmuch as it would be difficult or impossible to duplicate it satisfactorily, and inasmuch as it is already available and in good operating condition, why not employ the human nervous system itself for the purpose in view? Why not, in short, turn to careful introspection?

That question is a difficult one to push aside. Clearly, there is a sort of natural affinity between the motor theory of consciousness and the kind of introspection here suggested. Seen in the perspective of the motor theory, introspectional behaviorism becomes particularly comprehensible and compelling. It becomes a straightforward investigation of "external" stimulus-response contingencies. Data regarding those contingencies may be obtained by objective report or by subjective; but both kinds of report are describing precisely the same realm of nature.

It happens to be my personal conviction that the motor theory of consciousness is very probably valid. It is plausible not only in terms of introspective reality, but in terms of the basic plan of the nervous system as well (cf. Sperry 1952). There exists a reasonable amount of evidence in its favor (McGuigan 1966); and the evidence often cited most vigorously against it, that of the lack of effect of curare drugs upon thought and perception, is ill-founded (Smith 1964).

If the motor theory is indeed essentially true, the picture just drawn becomes veridical. We have at hand an elegant model for behavior and a potent technique for its study. Unfortunately, however, there is no denying that the motor theory is at least controversial. It is sometimes argued, for example, that the sequence, *efferent impulse--muscular response–afferent return*, might actually be short-circuited, so to speak, to become the simpler one, *efferent impulse–afferent return*; and there is in fact some fragmentary evidence that the requisite cross-pathways may exist in the brain (cf. Taub, Bacon, and Berman 1965). Admittedly, if a "central theory" of the sort thus implied (or of any other sort) should turn out to be correct, the picture that has been limned here would become somewhat more involved. *C'est,* however, *la vie:* things are not always neat. What is truly important is that the picture would not be altered in any basic way. Perception, thought, imagination, dreams, emotions, and wishes would still remain as incontestably physical events; they would still give rise to conscious experience; the conscious experience would still simply "happen," as does sensation; and the individual would still be quite able to report those internal events which are of fundamental significance in filling out the stimulus-response narrative. In short, if the motor theory of consciousness is not actually valid, it might—for present purposes—just as well be.

Summary

On the basis of the definitions abstracted by the previous chapters, and of a brief historical review, it is suggested that psychology has been, and remains, the science of the nature, causes, and effects of conscious experience—conscious experience being specified always in terms of the stimulus situations instigating it. Its consequent relationship to biology is explored, and its essential autonomy is emphasized.

Finally, the somewhat remarkable insistence of modern psychology on avoiding the whole topic of conscious experience is examined. It is concluded that that insistence is unreasonable, and that a more defensible and productive approach to the subject matter of psychology would be afforded by a methodology described as "introspectional behaviorism."

REFERENCES

Attneave, F. 1962. "Perception and Related Areas." In: Koch, S. (ed.) ; 1962; *Psychology: a Study of a Science,* Volume 4; McGraw-Hill, New York.

Boring, E. G. 1932. "The Physiology of Consciousness." *Science, 75,* 32–39.

Burt, C. 1962. "The Concept of Consciousness." *Brit. J. Psychol., 53,* 229–242.

Carnap, R. 1956. "The Methodological Character of Theoretical Concepts." In: Feigl, H., and M. Scriven (eds.) ; *Minnesota Studies in the Philosophy of Science,* Volume I: *The Foundations of Science and the Concepts of Psychology and Psychoanalysis*; University of Minnesota Press, Minneapolis.

Feigl, H. 1959. "Philosophical Embarrassments of Psychology." *Amer. Psychologist, 14,* 115–128.

Gibson, E. J., and J. J. Gibson. 1950. "The Identifying Response; A Study of a Neglected Form of Learning." *Amer. Psychologist, 5,* 276 (abstract).

Giorgi, A. 1967. "A Phenomenological Approach." *Rev. of Existential Psychol. and Psychiatry, 7,* 106–118.

Homme, L. E. 1965. "Perspectives in Psychology: XXIV. Control of Coverants, the Operants of the Mind." *Psychol. Record, 15,* 501–511.

Koch, S. 1964. "Psychology and Emerging Conceptions of Knowledge as Unitary." In: Wann, T. W. (ed.) ; *Behaviorism and Phenomenology: Contrasting Bases for Modern Psychology*; University of Chicago Press, Chicago.

Lashley, K. S. 1958. "Cerebral Organization and Behavior."
    In: Solomon, H. C., S. Cobb, and W. Penfield (eds.);
    The Brain and Human Behavior: Volume 36, *Research
    Publications of the Association for Research in Nerv-
    ous and Mental Disease;* Williams and Wilkins, Balti-
    more. Also, reprinted in: Beach, F. A., D. O. Hebb,
    C. T. Morgan, and H. W. Nissen (eds.); 1960; *The
    Neuropsychology of Lashley;* McGraw-Hill, New York.
MacLeod, R. B. 1964. "Phenomenology: A Challenge to Ex-
    perimental Psychology." In: Wann, T. W. (ed.); *Be-
    haviorism and Phenomenology: Contrasting Bases for
    Modern Psychology;* University of Chicago Press, Chi-
    cago.
May, R. (ed.). 1961. *Existential Psychology,* Random
    House, New York.
May, R. 1967. *Psychology and the Human Dilemma.* Van
    Nostrand; Princeton, New Jersey.
McGuigan, F. J. 1966. *Thinking: Studies of Covert Lan-
    guage Processes.* Appleton-Century-Crofts, New York.
Rogers, C. R. 1964. "Toward a Science of the Person." In:
    Wann, T. W. (ed.); *Behaviorism and Phenomenology:
    Contrasting Bases for Modern Psychology;* University
    of Chicago Press, Chicago.
Smart, J. J. C. 1963. *Philosophy and Scientific Realism.* Hu-
    manities Press, New York.
Smith, K. 1951. "Psychology and the Concept of 'Life.' "
    Psychol. Rev., 58, 330–331.
Smith, K. 1958a. "On the Interrelationships Among Organi-
    zation, Motivation, and Emotion." *Canad. J. Psychol.,
    12,* 69–73.
Smith, K. 1958b. "The Naturalistic Conception of Life."
    Amer. Scientist, 46, 413–423.
Smith, K. 1964. "Curare Drugs and Total Paralysis." *Psy-
    chol. Rev., 71,* 77–79.
Sperry, R. W. 1952. "Neurology and the Mind-Brain Prob-
    lem." *Amer. Scientist, 40,* 291–312.
Taub, E., R. C. Bacon, and A. J. Berman. 1965. "Acquisition
    of a Trace-Conditioned Avoidance Response After

Deafferentation of the Responding Limb." *J. Comp. and Physiol. Psychol., 59,* 275–299.

Washburn, M. F. 1922. "Introspection as an Objective Method." *Psychol. Rev., 29,* 89–112.

Zener, K. 1958. "The Significance of Experience of the Individual for the Science of Psychology." In: Feigl, H., M. Scriven, and G. Maxwell (eds.); *Minnesota Studies in the Philosophy of Science,* Volume II: *Concepts, Theories, and the Mind-Body Problem;* University of Minnesota Press, Minneapolis.

NOTES

The portions of this chapter especially concerned with "introspectional behaviorism" were discussed, in 1967, in a Hospital Lecture at the Veterans Administration Hospital at Salisbury, North Carolina, and before the Psychology Colloquium of Ohio University. In view of what is said in the chapter, a recent statement by Herbert Feigl (*The "Mental" and the "Physical": The Essay and a Postscript,* University of Minnesota Press, 1967) is of interest. Thus, among other things, Feigl remarks both that "strange as it may sound at first, it is possible that by doing introspective-phenomenological description of immediate experience, we are in effect (though we are hardly ever aware of it) doing also a bit of (very crude, vague, and preliminary) brain physiology" (page 149); and "as soon as the *peripheralistic* type of behaviorism . . . is supplemented by theories about the *central* states and processes within the organism, . . . it is on its way to the kind of physicalism which forms the frame-hypothesis of the present philosophical analysis" (pages 154–155). Both statements seem closely consonant with what has been said here.

ACKNOWLEDGMENTS

A NUMBER OF individuals have been kind enough to discuss or to correspond about portions of the foregoing monograph with me, at one time or another, and I wish to express my gratitude to them. Professors Lewis R. Aiken, Jr., Warren Ashby, Irenaes A. Burch, Carroll C. Pratt, Donald H. Ford, Christian P. Heinlein, Kenneth MacCorquodale, Robert Radlow, William S. Ray, Martin Roeder, and Hugh B. Urban have been especially helpful, as was the late Professor Karl Zener. Naturally, however, none of these men is to be held responsible for what the monograph has finally become.

Work has been assisted by research leaves provided in 1961 and 1968 by the University of North Carolina at Greensboro, and by a grant from the Faculty Research Council of that university. During several summers, Connecticut College and Mitchell College (both of New London, Connecticut) have kindly furnished library or study facilities. To all of these institutions, I wish to express my appreciation.